The P

MW00581422

The Poems
of Hafez

Translated into English by
Reza Ordoubadian

Foreword by
Shahriar Zangeneh

Ibex Publishers
Bethesda, Maryland

The Poems of Hafez

translated into English by Reza Ordoubadian

Copyright © 2006 Reza Ordoubadian

Miniature on front cover courtesy of Freer Gallery of Art.

Manufactured in Canada

∞ The paper used in this book meets the minimum requirements of the American National Standard for Information Services – Permanence of Paper for Printed Library Materials, ANSI Z39.48 1984

IBEX Publishers, Inc.
Post Office Box 30087
Bethesda, Maryland 20824 USA
Telephone: 301-718-8188
Facsimile: 301-907-8707
www.ibexpublishers.com

Library of Congress Cataloging-in-Publication Data

Hāfiz, 14th cent.
[Dīvān. English. Selections]
The poems of Hafez / translated into English by Reza Ordoubadian ; foreword by Shahriar Zangeneh.
p. cm.
Translated from Persian.
Includes bibliographical references and index.
ISBN 1-58814-019-9 (alk. paper)
1. Ordoubadian, Reza.
PK6465.Z32 O73 2005
891/.5511 22
2005047464

For
Margaret, Parri, Kimi, Hossein, and David
and
Other members of the Ordoubadi Clan

TABLE OF CONTENTS

ACKNOWLEDGMENTS

I am grateful to Shahriar Zangeneh for his untiring efforts to help me with advice, encouragement, research and kind words. His final editing of the manuscript has been invaluable. This book could not become a reality without his unselfish gift of friendship and editorial skills.

I am grateful to Mr. Baha-al-Din Khorramshahi for writing his magnificent two volume critical commentary on the *ghazals* of Hafez. When in trouble, I ran to his books for enlightenment.

My thanks to Margaret for undertaking to proof the final draft of this book so carefully and with so much dedication, and for her voice in my head all these many years to do the translations.

FOREWORD

Hafez, although born some six hundred years ago in southern Iran, is a contemporary and universal poet. Those familiar with the Persian language have made him the culture's most read and revered literary figure. His verse not only gives a panoramic insight into the culture of Persia but also a window into understanding the universal soul. His turn of phrase has enriched the Persian lexicon and, even more than Shakespeare in English, has entered everyday language. His mesmerizing arrangement of simple words is sumptuous, melodic and symphonic.

Hafez is a matchmaker who reconciles the inner earthly needs, wants and desires with society's dictates. Friedrich Rückert, the nineteenth century German scholar, phrases it: "Hafez's poetry, looks sensual and is supra-sensual; when he seems to talk about things spiritual, his spirituality is sensual as his sensuality is spiritual, and it is impossible to disentangle the two levels of meaning, which belongs to each other."

Hafez's verse is a multifaceted gem that reflects different shades of light according to the reader's state of mind. The very same lines may be uplifting, melancholic, introspective, inspirational or irreligiously religious. They are, however, always sensual. The language has various levels of meaning. Religiosity and apostasy or subservience and disobedience can be read in the same line. This was Hafez's way of bypassing contemporary prohibitions on expression of certain thoughts or feelings.

Many have previously attempted to translate Hafez. Meaning, melody or spirit has been conveyed, but never all three. More recently Hafez has been used as a nominal inspirational anchor by modern English language poets. Reza Ordoubadian's translations achieve that lovely balance of being true to the feeling, music and letter of the original, and at the same time employing a very fluent and contemporary English.

Ordoubadian, having been born in Iran, being well-read in Persian poetry and prose, and having taught English literature in America, has the perfect résumé for a translator of Hafez. He understands the nuances of Hafez's language and thought—that they are as relevant and universal today as the day they were originally penned. In these translations, Hafez, one of humanity's greatest poets, becomes easier accessible in a more authentic and faithful version to the English language reader.

— Shahriar Zangeneh
Washington, DC 2006

INTRODUCTION

Preface

How does one fall in love with Hafez, or any other artist, for that matter? Hafez is one of the principal foundations of the Persian culture, someone whose word is not just experienced on the surface, but whose word provides an inner light, a sense of otherness, that permeates the way of life of the people who experience it. Hafez is, with Rumi, Saadi, and Ferdowsi, one of the rare souls who has molded the thinking of the Iranian people and Persian speakers all over the world for six centuries. One need only go to the traditional music of Iran to notice how often the poems of this fourteenth century poet (1325?-1389? A.D.) are used as the lyrics for the most delicate airs of the Iranian people. No one who has lived any period of time in Iran escapes exposure to Hafez because he is everywhere in the culture: in the market places and in the streets, on the radio stations and among lovers, between husbands and wives, children at school and taxi drivers. I was on a Fulbright grant in Iran in 1970, and as my taxi weaved through the streets of Tehran, the driver began mumbling something very musical, which I could not hear clearly. I asked what he was singing, and with delighted laughter he said, "Nothing (*heechi*, *agha*)! Just reciting some ghazals of Hafez." He said he was depressed, and reciting Hafez always gave him a boost. "Oh, I can recite a couple of dozens of ghazals," he answered when I asked how many lines of Hafez he had in memory. "I just learned them." He had only an elementary education, and whatever he knew of Hafez, he had picked up from the market places and street corners. He informed me that his father knew two books by heart: The Holy Koran and the Ghazals of Hafez. I do not question the veracity of the claim, for it is likely that he did.

I myself grew up in Tehran and can vouch for the attraction of this grand poet, whose ghazals never exceed fifteen lines, mostly of seven or eight. What was his hold on me, I have often wondered, and now, at the latter part of my life, I think I have an answer, an answer most people might give.

I fell in love with Hafez when I was in my late teens; of course, I had no choice in the matter: anyone who had any claim to intellect and knowledge had to love Hafez, and I pretended I did. I would have made myself the object of ridicule by declaring that I found the man boring and unintelligible. Yet, I convinced myself that I did love him and recited a few lines from memory to my father, who was a great admirer of the poet and whose collected works, *Divan-e Hafez*, he kept in the middle drawer of his desk at home, where he also stored boxes of gourmet yellow raisons and Turkish delight; he had a copy of the book at his office, too. Here was a merchant of some success, who cared enough to keep the poems of a distant poet close by for consolation and pleasure. Before I was twenty, I had collected a number of beautifully illustrated and bound volumes of the poet's Divan in my limited library, but I never bought a single one of those copies in my collection: they had been given me by family members and friends, each aware that I probably did have a copy, but a gift of Hafez was precious and an expression of love. One copy I have kept to this day; I brought it with me to the United States when I was studying at Duke University. It is the selected ghazals of Hafez in small print with a very skimpy introduction, but gloriously gaudy illustrations in the style of master miniaturists. My volume is a lithographic printing in the four-color process. A woman friend at the university gave it to me the day I was leaving Iran—not to return, although I did not know it at the time.

This early love affair diminished as I became immersed in my studies and as I tried to remove pretense from the agenda of my life (how prophetic that Hafez, I realized later, is a debunker of pretenses and hypocrisies). My early flirtation with Hafez was derailed by my introduction to Western culture and civilization when I discovered writers from Anglo-Saxon to twentieth century literature. In one of my classes in American Literature, when we were studying Ralph Waldo Emerson, my professor mentioned, privately, that Emerson had been influenced by a Persian poet named Hafez. Did I know the poet? For sure, I did, and the next day I brought my illustrated Hafez to show Dr. Ghodes. "Fine," he said. "Why don't you see if you can find a seminar paper in this?" At that time, professors were like gods, and I accepted the assignment reluctantly, although privately miffed that my professor was probably trying to help me by assigning a paper topic on a familiar subject: such patronizing! So be it, I thought, although I would rather have written a "pure" seminar paper on American literature. The result was a short, twenty-page paper on the reputation of Hafez in the west and Emerson's use of his imagery and metaphors. That was it: the rest of my life until very recently has been spent dealing with English literature and linguistics, no mention of Hafez at all. I do not think I had taken my "gaudy" Hafez volume in hand in thirty years, but when I did, it had the power of magic, and I became "pregnant" with a child inside my head that had to be born. My wife did not help the matter by constantly asking me when I was going to do my Hafez project, which I never thought I had. Not that I had not mentioned Hafez during my academic years. On occasion, just to impress colleagues and students, I would make references to this "revered Iranian poet," but, again, it was more an affectation than a true believer's honest statement. These years, I have come to call the arid years!

At a Jungian workshop in 1995 I casually mentioned my interest in Hafez to Robert Bly; at the time, he was considering a translation of Hafez himself. Later, I wrote him, asking if he would care to work with me on the project. He was not interested at that time, but I decided to read Hafez to see what it was that I was really proposing to do. I certainly had forgotten the few verses that I had trusted to my memory during my youth, and I had not systematically studied the man and his work. I took my "gaudy" Hafez and began reading it. If I had fallen in love with him during my early years out of compulsion and then divorced him for many decades from my mind willfully, now I began to fall in love with Hafez in a true sense. He was magnificent, and I even tried some Jungian interpretation of a few of his poems. By 1999, I had read a number of collections of his works and had consulted Sir Edward Browne, A. J. Arberry, and others, and my interest was peaking. On a whim, I translated ten of his ghazals, and early in 2001, I sent them to The Iranian.com—just for the "heck" of it. They were published immediately, and the results were unexpected. I received a number of e-mails from people whom I never knew, among them one person, who has since become my mentor and friend. Shahriar Zangeneh, whom I have not had the pleasure of meeting yet, wrote a short note that really inspired me. We exchange e-mail several times a week and, on occasion, several times a day. He thought I should finish my translations and publish the book. Here is the book, but this time I am "truly" in love with "His High Majesty, Hafez," as Zangeneh calls him, and would like to share my love with anyone who cares to read these pages, but a word of caution: what I have done is a poetic translation, and that is what this book should be considered. If anyone desires to find a literal translation, he will not find it in this volume. I have translated the poems and not interpreted them. That is the province of the reader and the literary critic.

The Process of Translation

How does one translate Hafez? Many have tried, some with a measure of success, but to my knowledge, there has not been a collected number of ghazals published in the west which compares with Edward Fitzgerald's *Rubaiyat* of *Omar Khayyam*. In India, in the Arabic speaking countries, and in Turkey, Hafez's works have been indeed translated with great success, but not into English. One does not just take a dictionary in one hand and the Divan in the other to match words in Persian with those in English: this will be counter to any linguistic intuition, necessary to produce meaningful language. Translation at best is a marker because matching of words in itself is an impossible task; one theory holds that synonymy is a myth and that each word in each language has its own life-force and set of meanings. Even in the same language, there is a problem dealing properly with such words as the English word "fatherly" and its supposed synonym "paternal." True, they both refer to a male parent, but in actual usage, especially when they are used in metaphors, the two words prove to be quite different. We can say, "Our Heavenly Father," but hardly, "Our Heavenly Patron!" The two words "glad" and "happy" have a vague similarity, but are not really synonyms, as is true with the Persian words *"khoshroo"* and *"zeebaa."* Certainly no Persian speaker will agree that they are the same words, although they both refer to some sort of vague sense of "beauty." So, even in the same language it is difficult to match words indicating the same referent.

Besides, words are meaningless until they are strung together in a quantum in the form of sentences. We will say, "The man told the woman," and turn around and change the order of the same words, and we will have two different sentences with two entirely different meanings: "The woman told the man." This becomes amplified as we try to translate Persian, which combines words together in a synthesis and agglutination to make a sentence. In Persian, it does not make any difference to say *"be oo goftam"* or *"goftam be oo"* (I told him/her and only rarely, him, I told) because that element (enclitic) "-am" specifies the subject, and there is no need to worry about the position of subject, verb, or object in the sentence, unlike in English where position is a large part of marking case.

Imagine trying to accommodate an analytic language (English) to a synthetic language (Persian) in translation. The task of a translator becomes more interesting!

Words at best are markers of abstract concepts and ideas inside the human mind. Individually, they more "concretely" reflect what we mean. However, in combination, there are all sorts of missing parts and missing notions that we must provide, both as a speaker and as a hearer. If we were to indicate all these markers, a simple expression would take five minutes to say. A sentence has a meaning as a form, like the form of a statue; remove the form, all that remains is scattered metal and raw material, as words are. However, when we put words into the form of a sentence, we move away from the concrete and face a higher degree of abstraction because those missing parts must be provided by other human activities, such as culture, history, and the arts of the particular society that uses the language. For example, there are twelve musical modes in Persian and only three in western music. Since language is closely connected with music (sounds we make with our oral cavity are musical notations), when we produce Persian sentences, unaware, we make use of these modalities. The English language uses three. Then, when one translates a sentence from Persian to English, how does one account for this aspect of language? Nothing much can be done here except to improvise and hope for understanding. This is a problem in translating a simple sentence: when we move from prose to poetry, music becomes even more important. Hafez uses not only musical terminology, but he employs musical devices to create his songs. No wonder they lend themselves so beautifully to singing, as the traditional music of Iran will show. How often have we heard Wordsworth or even Shakespeare set to popular music, recorded and performed in all the various venues of the media? (True, a number of Shakespearean plays have been made into operas, but they are hardly the direct words of the bard). With this new introduction of sound the single, more or less concrete, word used in a poetic phrase becomes even more abstract. Reading a poem in any language requires more than just the knowledge of the literal meaning of the words. It requires a deep sense of and an intuitive grasp of elements in philosophy, history, and psychology, even though the reader of the poem may not be aware of them at all. At this level of language use, we approach the final abstraction: the meaning of the language no longer depends on single words or the form of sentences, or even discourse, but on tacit understanding of deep, hidden, often subconscious notions by the user of the language. This is true not only in the case of the so called educated class, but it is a universally occurring phenomenon, by degrees, for any native speaker of the language, to which my taxi driver friend in Tehran testified. At this abstract level, we must use all our human possibilities to see into the heart of the poem and make sense of the jumble of words. Here we come to such elements of language as metaphors, imagery, and intentional ambiguities that a poet incorporates into his poems. We know for a fact that Hafez is variously considered by people as the "divine bard," a "libertine," an "atheist lout," worthy of flogging, or a man of supreme spiritual attainment who beckons us to join him in the celebration of life through both wine from the tavern and wine from the vat of spirit. I think he is all of these, an Epicurean and a mystic, who sees the mystical gnosis through Epicurean sensibilities. Of course, age must play a role: I am confident that Hafez's later poems are much more sedate than the ones he wrote as a young man, and if by any chance, someone were able to make a chronology of his poetry with ample documentation, this evolution would be obvious.

At this point in language use, we move from the concrete-ness of a single word back to the abstraction that exists before a concept becomes words. In other words, poetry comes closest to the abstraction of the poet's mind, and in that abstraction the poet shares his mind with that of the reader. This is the source of the love affair: we see the world as the poet before us has seen it, urging an equilibrium between the worldly and the other worldly, between sensuality and spirituality, equations that cannot be altered because if one side of the equation is aborted, the other side cannot exist in this dialectic. If the same people who speak the language of Hafez extrapolate such divergent meanings from his poems—often, we translate poetry to prose in our minds to make it more concrete for understanding—how does one take the elements of Hafez and find the right concrete words in English and find the right forms in which to translate the abstraction of Hafez in Persian into an abstraction of Hafez in English? The easiest part is dealing with his dialectics because we have examples of it in English literature in abundance.

Obviously, poetry uses many of the devices of music, and to create his music, a poet must fashion devices of his own that are available to him in the form of sounds and the harmony of his text. One of the essentials in music is repetition; as a matter of fact, the human psyche receives a great deal of pleasure hearing patterns that are repeated, in sound or in sight. Poets often use the same sound or the same phrases to create music, the most obvious being refrains. However, a poem requires less obvious means of music-making, such as repeating the same sound at the beginning, middle or the end of words in the same line of a poem; this device is called alliterative structuring. Reading the Persian version of Ghazal 71 (Khorramshahi numbering) will illustrate the point. I will quote line 1 in transliteration: *"jaan be jamaaleh jaanaan meyleh jahaan nadaarad."*

The sounds /j/ and /n/ have been repeated four times each, not to mention the repetition of /aa/. It is impossible to find four English words with the same sound that will provide the appropriate meaning for this half line of Hafez's poetry. This is just one example of hundreds of instances of alliteration in the ghazals.

Then, there is the problem of idiom and ambiguity. One reason Hafez's poetry can be read on so many different levels is that he chooses words in his sentences that may have multiple meanings, all valid according to how the reader reacts to them. This poses a great stricture on the translator because ambiguity is not something that can be easily translated from one language to another. In English, I can say, "I am painting a house," which may mean either I am painting the picture of a house or using a brush and paint to cover a real house, my house. It can also mean, "I have hired someone to do it," or "I am doing it myself." Thus, there are four different meanings hidden in one form. This sentence cannot be translated into Persian in one single, parallel sentence to mean both intentions; instead, we will have two sentences. 1) *"khoona-mo rang mi-zan-am"* or 2) *"khoona-mo rang mi-zan-and."* There is no ambiguity here because there are two sentences to describe two concepts, and a Persian speaker will not be faced with any choice of meaning. Persian syntax requires enclitics (*pasvand*) to indicate person and number, whereas in English position determines those. No doubt about it in the mind of a Persian speaker who hears the sentence with /-am/: it is *I* who does the painting, with /-and/ it is **they** (someone other than *I*) who paints. Hafez devilishly does this often. In Ghazal 88, line 4, he says, *"bas aabe roo keh baa khaakeh rah baraameezad"* (much water from the face [albeit, eyes]/honor that mixes with the dust of the road).The phrase *"aabeh roo"* can be translated either as real water with which one washes his face or "honor." It is essential that the reader of the poem understand this distinction and this possibility of double entendre; otherwise, understanding will be superficial. Again, what does a translator do to render this lovely ambiguity into English? No way!

Of course, there is also the problem of innuendo, approximation, and allusions, sometimes in the form of metaphors, often pure references to events or people. In Ghazal 79, line 3, where from the word "*eshteghagh*" (derivation) we have "*shafagh*" (aurora) and "*shafaghat*." (compassion), both used in a special way that only the context will clarify their usage-meanings. In the metaphor of "*deedehye mashoogheh baazeh man*" in Ghazal 208, line 2, one can only hint at the metaphor of "a gaze that makes love and roves!" But it could also mean "lustful eyes," "roving eyes," or the "eyes of discernment." How un-poetic in English and how deliciously meaningful in Hafez! Often times, also, we have the problem of approximation: there is no word for "*mohtaseb*" in English, and I had to make up a word, for which, variously, I have used "judge," "sheriff," "bailiff," or "jailer," none very satisfactory. There are references to Haji Ghavaam or Khajeh and other historical figures that will be alien to an English speaking audience, even modern speakers of Persian; these names are allusions that have a wealth of historical meaning in the life of poetry, lost, if not recognized. Another example is in Ghazal 239, line 5, where there is a reference to *Sheerin* and *Farhaad*, a pair of legendary lovers whose love is doomed before it starts: the story is the Persian equivalent of Tristan and Isolde; but the word "*Sheerin*" could mean "sweetness" or the name of this mythological lover. Hafez means to be ambiguous or, even, to use both meanings at the same time (Sweet *Sheerin*), but in English such a rendering will not be possible.

By far, the most intriguing, and at the same time daunting, problem is grammar. Persian, fortuitously, lacks gender or case distinction in personal pronouns. One of the achievements of Hafez is that he uses an idea without committing himself to gender; it is only on rare occasions that he definitely means masculine by the generic third person singular pronoun "*oo*." Therefore, one can read Hafez comfortably in Persian without being hampered by homophobia or even an awareness that Hafez may mean masculine while our minds read the text feminine. Then, in English, mischief shouts out for clarification. The Persian "*oo*" can be translated either as "he" or "she" in abstraction, but in context there is a definite delineation of "*oo*" by Hafez. The matter becomes even more troublesome when we know a ghazal is a mystical expression of Hafez about the divine and that the beloved is God and the relationship is one of pure spirit. If the translator uses "she" in the text, it will directly contradict the English cultural semantics that refers to God as "He." Notwithstanding feminist wishes, Jesus refers to God as *"abba,"* in Aramaic meaning father (Daddy, really), and the Lord's Prayer starts as "Our Father Who art in heaven...." Two thousand years of divine maleness has firmly established itself in western culture so that we refer to God as "He" (not She or He/She) even though we know God, as the creator of all, has no gender. So, where do I stand in translating this word? If I use "she," which will fit beautifully and make the poem, on one level, purely a love song, then, when we go to deep structure of the semantic features, this will be a totally inappropriate use of the language. If, on the other hand, I use "he," I stand to be asked, "Was Hafez a homosexual, and the beloved, a man?" An absurd and irrelevant question, but one that is there and might even put off some people. I have tried to get around this problem by unfortunate and repetitive use of such words as "lover" or "beloved," but how dull it is to be using the same word over and over! An example of such impossibility is to be found in Ghazal 187, line 4. This, too, is a major problem for a translator. Ghazal 63 is so full of allusions and imagery that it is virtually untranslatable in a faithful manner. Then, there is the phonological transposition and the interplay of words. In Ghazal 232, line 5, we have *"dar on chaman keh botaan dasteh aasheghaan geerand"* (In that meadow where idols take the hand of the lovers) which is paired off in the second half of the line with *"garat ze dast bar aayad neghaar-e man baashi"* (If possible, you become my sweetheart). In this line Hafez uses /d/ and /n/ and /g/ as alliterative devices, but also the sense of the first half of the line is lost on the second half when translated into English. It makes perfect sense in Persian and is, indeed, very musical; in English, it sounds trite and naïve.

No poetry can exist without metaphor; as a matter of fact, I suggest that no art can exist without metaphor. That which seethes in the mind of the artist and must be born cannot easily take shape in inadequate containers, words that are barely markers of the abstraction inside the head. As a matter of fact, words are metaphors, if we expand the notion of metaphor to include symbols and signs. The notion of a table is not the same notion for every one: the English word "table" is only a container into which we collect the various notions of "table" and use it for the sake of convenience; in its way, any word is an abstraction, but on a much lower level of thinking. Ferdinand de Saussure suggests, and later Leonard Bloomfield amplifies on it, that any given word is a triad of a notion in the mind, a sound symbol in the mouth, and a non-linguistic object. The broad implication of triad is that only the symbol (word) remains constant, and we can manipulate it in various ways. For example, we have a notion of "table-ness" and an object-table outside our heads, but we have multiple words to express the relationship in the many languages in the world. However, it is *possible* to alter the notion in the head, even the non-linguistic object, with words. We change our minds all the time, and according to the Heisenberg principle, when we identify an object with a word (observe it), we alter its nature. Hafez does this masterfully by switching the meaning of words. For example, *"zaahed"* is ordinarily used to identify a virtuous person. For Hafez, it is the opposite, a hypocrite, a pretender. The reader must adjust his thinking to this new meaning of the word, thus both the non-linguistic object and the notion in the head are altered. The question is, how does a translator accommodate this switch in the limited translation-space he has? It is the symbol (the word "table," in this case) that makes the non-linguistic object available to describe the notion in the head. In this sense, a word is a sort of metaphor. However, complicated abstraction inside the creative mind of the artist requires a way of expression that is not available through simple words. The poet paints a word-picture in his effort to unveil the picture of his mind, but it never approaches the reality of the picture contained in the mind. Our everyday language is replete with metaphors and imagery, and we could not really communicate without them. How can I say "The apple I am eating is sweet"? Sweet is not graspable at all, but if I said "The apple I am eating is sweet sugar," I have made a very concrete statement about the nature of the apple. Hafez often talks about his wine as "tulip" or even "rose" and "ruby." The clarity we can envision by ruby is such that we can understand the kind of wine Hafez is referring to; this is always contrasted by the phrase "lees drinkers," where the wine is full of sediment and only the Sufi and the initiate drink it. However, metaphors, like idioms, are culture bound and cannot be readily translated. Hafez considers "the arch of the brows" as "a bow" and the beloved's "eye lashes" as "arrows" that can be shot to pierce the heart of the beloved to wound him. This imagery is very difficult to convey in English, unless one can find a similar metaphor to substitute for the original one. Then, the criticism will follow that, in doing so, the translator has gone too far astray.

Fortunately, most images are profoundly connected to the same universal human thinking faculty, and there is reasonable parity in this matter from culture to culture. Awareness of archetypal metaphors in one culture and language can be carried over to another. On the most superficial level, Hafez's ghazals deal with the worldly satisfaction of human appetites. He seems to have a keen eye for beautiful faces and an appreciation of the "flirtation" of the beloved, a word that he uses frequently (*naaz, kereshmeh*, and such). One can be quite satisfied with his worldly wine and beloveds—even appreciate Hafez's rarified sensuality. It seems to me that Hafez reached a tremendous individuation and discernment; that is, if we are to talk about the divine and the mystical, our starting point must be the physical. It is in the real flesh-and-blood lovers and consummation of love that we begin our initiation into the ranks of the elect. Hafez argues that the transcendent can be only understood through the flesh because flesh gives spirit a house, and an understanding of the nature of the house is imperative for an understanding of the content, the spirit. Not for a moment do I think Hafez considers his debauchery a terrible state of mind. On the contrary, it is from there that one slowly approaches a window at the end of the room and very slowly looks through the opening to see the other side. Without this flesh and blood awareness, spiritual awareness is at best difficult, at worst, misunderstood.

On the first level of writing, Hafez provides the reader a table of delights to be consumed, experienced, and enjoyed, but one cannot remain in this place of delight for long. One must move on for better understanding of the world on the other side of the window. Therefore, the second level of expression is a painting of the transcendent. Ordinary wine becomes an element of God, beloved is the divine Person, and *"Peereh Moghan"* or "Tavern Keeper," a manifestation of the divine. Without the literal tavern, understanding the metaphorical tavern is impossible. No wonder Hafez has been considered both a "lout," ready to corrupt the minds of men and "a spiritual," who is conversant with the divine through his art! He is both, of course, and unless we see the whole of the poet, we will only have access to a part of his mind.

Fortunately, there are English poets who have a similar mind set. Keats considers this metaphor of window in his idea of "negative capability," and Wordsworth talks about the attainment of the mystical through exposure of the body to the physical (nature). In this sense, then, my task as a translator becomes easier than I had anticipated. Not that I have substituted English metaphors for the metaphors of Hafez, but my awareness of English poetry makes it easier to deal with the task of translation with foreknowledge.

As the reader can see, the task of a translator is a complex one: he must be faithful to the text of the original language while making sense in the language into which he is translating. The lines in the English verse may not be immediately recognizable when compared with the Persian original, yet a closer look will definitely show that one is the translation of the other. Of course, Hafez's ghazals are highly structured with definite metrics and prosodic devices. I have opted to forgo such strictures in favor of faithfulness to the original word. It would be unproductive to translate Hafez, using traditional English prosody and still remain faithful to him. My translations are poetry, but not traditionally structured. I have read enough translations from Persian into English to be convinced that no translator should attempt to imitate the prosody of one language in another. Just looking at the matter of alliteration will show how such an attempt will fail. If I had done so, I would have been a slave of Hafez's metrics and then, doubly, a slave of the English prosody: my translations try to reflect Hafez's music without using Hafez's devices.

Poesy of Hafez

Persian poetry enjoys such a variety of form and structure that discussing the style of even one poet will require an extended exploration. Since this book is a translation of the ghazals of Hafez, a few words should suffice here.

Structurally, as in Anglo-Saxon poetry (e.g. *Beowulf*), all traditional Persian poetic lines are divided into two half-lines with a caesura in the middle. I suggest that most Persian poetry, as the traditional poetry of any other culture, was composed not so much to be recited as sung—even without accompanying musical instruments—either as chanting or straight singing. The caesura technically affords a singer time to catch his breath—certainly most singers were men—in the middle of the line and then continue to the second half; Persian music is commonly in minor key and uses quarter-tone notes and trill, the rapid alternation of two tones either a whole or a half tone apart in the voice, requiring a great amount of exhaling breath.

Some scholars use the term sonnet—from *sonata*, meaning a song—to refer to ghazal. Ghazals are certainly *sonata*, but this is not exactly an accurate naming because sonnet has a definite form of fourteen lines, both in the Petrarchan and Shakespearean forms. An English sonnet is divided into three quatrains and an ending couplet; a Petrarchan sonnet is composed of two sections, the first with eight lines and the second with six. They both require definite rhyming schemes, which are consistent and syllabic. However, Hafez composes his ghazals in a varying number of lines and often uses whole words—one could consider them as word refrains—for his rhyming, which come at the end of all second half-lines and the two halves of the first line, a good reason for the editors of Hafez in Persian to arrange his poetry alphabetically and according to these end-words.

The narrative voice in both English and Latin sonnets remains somewhat constant, which allows the poet to propose a theme in the first section of a sonnet and then go to a conclusion in the second part. Hafez has a clever twist to his ghazals. He commonly uses at least two voices, one in the main body of the ghazal, with varying conversational or descriptive tones, the voice remaining constant, as if an observer is making comments and is not necessarily involved with the content of the poem. Yet, when the final couplet is reached, often the voice changes, and it is Hafez's turn to make a comment openly or be addressed by another mysterious voice, which could be the voice of his inner self, consciousness, or reason. I assume this device allows Hafez to say more than he is willing to say, at the same time escaping even a harsher censor from his critics. After all, when his voice is heard, it is all reason and circumspection. In the 202 ghazals that I have translated, rarely does Hafez leave himself open to criticism in the final couplet. If anything, he is self deprecatory and evasive.

Arrangement of the Poems

For a reason that I have never been able to ascertain, Hafez's poetry is arranged not according to the history of the poems or types of poetry, but according to a special rhyming scheme at the end of lines.* Unlike in English, where rhyming is a matter of matching sounds at the end of lines—or, internally—Persian poetry rhymes with whole words or morphological clusters; that is, either the same word or the same morpheme is repeated at the end of each line. Then, the poems that contain end-words with "*alef*" come first and those with "*yey*" come last, regardless of the date of composition or type. I am sure this has served readers very well through centuries, but since I have not used the rhyming scheme of Hafez, I did not feel bound to number the ghazals according to the traditional editorial systems. Moreover, the numbers vary from edition to edition. I have burdened the canon of Hafez yet with another

---

* Several attempts have been made to arrange the ghazals according to the date of their composition, none successfully. It is impossible to ascribe an accurate date to the ghazals, and only a few have internal historical references from which one may determine an approximate date.

numbering, from 1 to 202. However, to facilitate the reader's desire to compare the Persian version with the English, I have provided an index at the end of the book so that one may find the texts readily. For my purposes, I have used Baha-Al-Din Khorramshahi's numbers (*Hafez Nameh,* 2 vols. Sherkat-e Entesharat-e Elmi va Honari, Teheran: 1378) in this book. Four ghazals come from Parveez N. Khanlari (*Divan-e Hafez,* 2 volumes, Tehran: Sherkat-e Kharazmi, 1362.) The four are Ghazals 15, 52, 62, and 68 (my numbering system).

Additionally, I have provided a short list of pronunciation keys with examples in Persian and English as well as the International Phonetic Alphabetic system; I have used these graphemes when required by the use of Persian or Arabic words. Since Hafez repeats some of his key word/concepts through his ghazals, I have added a short list of these words for the reader's quick reference in Appendix I.

I have also a short bibliography at the end; additionally extensive notes are provided, which, I hope, will be useful both for reading the poems with facility and for venturing into some measure of interpretation by the readers.

— Reza Ordoubadian
July, 2006

VOWEL VALUES

Symbol Used	Persian Sample Word	IPA Symbol
a	ped*a*r (father)	ä
aa	j*a*n (body, soul)	α
e	z*e*ndeh (alive)	e
ee	b*ee*roon (outside)	i
o	g*o*ft (he said)	o
oo	d*oo*r (far away)	u

The Ghazals

One

Never! Not even the blaming vision of my foes:
    I cannot forsake my wine—nor my *rendi*.[1]
The way of the neo-*rendaan* leads to a single vale;
    I, in universal disrepute, why should I care?
Call me the king of the insane, a restive man:
    since my colossal ignorance exceeds all.
Mark your forehead with the blood of my heart:
    I'm your sacrificial offering, a heathen sot.
Have faith, proceed in the name of God
    so you will not know what a *naa-Darvish*[2] I.
O' wind! Blow my bloodied verse to my beloved,
    who has opened the vein of my life with her lash.
        If I drink my wine, who's hurt?
        I'm the keeper of my secret, aware of my time.

Two

Last dawn I told my story to the wind, my yearning;
    a voice declared, "Be secure in the grace of God."
Morning prayer, sighs at night: key to unlocking the treasure gates.
    Follow this path to be united with the object of love.
Can this mute pen reveal the secrets of love?
    It's the limits of expression to talk of longing.
Behold! Egyptian Joseph, drunk with the conceit of power:
    Ask of your father—where is hid the love of a son?
The cosmos, she shows little mercy for an old man's folly:
    Why ask for comfort? Why tie your hopes to it?
You, majestic eagle: how long will you crave for dry bones?[3]
    Pity! You cast your mantle upon those thankless men!
If any profit in this souk, the happy dervish possess it:
    Oh, God, make me rich with darvishi[4] and happiness.
        To the song of Hafez they flirt and dance:
        The black-eyed Kashmiris and the Turks of Samarkand.

Three

You hear a discerning voice: do not confound it.
    You are not discerning: there lies the rub.
My concern is not for this world—or the other;
    Blessed God! What temptations crowd our heads!
Who resides inside my weary heart?
    I remain silent, full of passion and fight!
Discord rules my heart: Oh, where are you musician!
    Sing your tune; bring harmony to this patrician.
Disinclined with the affairs of this world:
    only the beauty of your face opens my eyes
Bereft of sleep, heart breaking with empty thoughts,
    hung-over for a thousand nights! Where is the tavern?
I have desecrated the temple with my blood:
    if I'm given ablutions with the wine, why not?[5]
The reason our Master is kept in high esteem and dear, is that
    a fire unquenched lives eternally in our hearts.
What air the musician plays behind the scale with his harp?
    My life expires, yet my head is filled with airs!
        At dusk the voice of your love intones within my heart:
        the vastness of Hafez's chest still echoes with voices.

Four

The pretentious pseudo-ascetic![6] to our nature he is oblivious.
    However he portrays us, we're not perjured!
On the way, what comes to the disciple is blessing:
    in the straight path of truth, no one is lost!
However rook displays, my pawn plays:
    on the chess board of the rendaan—the king has no place.
This simple ceiling of heavens, sprinkled with patterns: its purpose?
    No wise man in the world is privy to it.
Oh, God! Your absolute immanence and wisdom in place:
    why all the hidden wounds? And, no time to sigh?
Our accountant misses the calculations entirely:
    in his book, nothing is entered for the sake of God.
Hold not back--your needs, nor your words:
    no need of pride, coyness, nor ceremonies in this house!
The pure of heart may knock at the tavern's[7] door:
    it's locked in the face of those meta-harlots![8]
A flaw in the fit? It's in our imperfect bodies, not the suit:
    your grace showers equally upon those who wear it.
I'm a slave of the tavern Master, whose favor is firm:
    that of the virtuous, sometimes it is there, sometimes not!
        It is Hafez's honor to spurn false places of honor:
        true lees drinking lovers do not care for position or honor!

Five

The fruit of the loom of existence is for naught,
    Bring wine: fruits of this world are for naught.
My heart and soul yearn to converse with the beloved:
    just an intention! My heart and my soul are for naught.
Do not beg for a shade from Sedreh and Toobaa;[9]
    a better look, my beloved: the soul is for naught.
True treasures come—through grace with no heart breaks;
    the price of paradise with works, it's for naught.
A few days in this world, and you are gone:
    rest with peace for a time; time is for naught.
O Saghi, we await at the shores of the sea of mortality:
    seize the moment; from lips to your mouth is for naught.
Do not rest, oh ascetic, assured of salvation:
    from your prayer rug to the wine cellar all is for naught!
My inner pain, my complaints, my heart's break
    obviously do not merit mentioning for naught!
        Hafez has gained a measure of good reputation, but,
        with real rendaan the measure of gain or loss is for naught!

Six

Sweet words I did hear the Elder of Canaan[10] sing:
    "The tale of separation from the beloved cannot be easily told."
The fable of the horrors of the resurrection our preacher sang:
    merely a metaphor of separation, if the truth be told.
Whom shall I ask for a sign from my absent voyager?
    Whatever the winged steed uttered was vainly told!
Alas! That unloving beloved, bereft of love,
    taking leave of the friends, how easily he told!
Hence, nothing but resignation,[11] and appreciation of the Master:
    my heart inured to pain, farewell to healing, I spoke.
"Ancient sorrows drown in agéd wine."
    "The seeds of blessedness is in this," the Old Planter[12] said.
"Do not write your words on shifting sand, even if expedient!"
    This riddle Solomon[13] to Zephyr told.
How can you be fooled by the fate at hand
    to fall to her deceits, who false stories told.
Stop this contention: the fortunate man
    accepted in his soul all that the beloved told.
        Who said Hafez returned because of your thoughts?
        Not me! He who said it, a calumny he told!

Seven

Life devoid of the face of lovers has no desire for life:[14]
    one lacking this one, certainly lacks the other one!
No one could clue me to a sign from my lover:
    either I live in the dark—or she shows no signs?
Each fragile night-dew in this path is a hundred flaming lakes:
    alas, this enigma cannot be painted with words!
I will not abandon my leisure—and rush.
    O caravan, settle down: no end's in sight!
That bent, ancient harp, singing delights of life:
    hearken to the ancient air, melody, your guide![15]
My heart, learn the way of rendaan from our sheriff:
    who dares accuse him to be tippled with wine?
The treasures of Midas, strewn to four winds,
    whisper to your ears, "No gold will stay!"
Vying with the candle? Hide your secrets from her:
    that saucy cut-head, holds no bars at her tongue!
        No one in the world holds a slave like Hafez:
        since a king like you no one beholds in life!

Eight

Creation! Before the light of creation dazzled chaos,
    Love was created—that set on fire the creation![16]
The dazzled light cannot burn the passive angel's heart:
    the lover set the burning human heart in that light.
Reason saw—desired to borrow a flicker of that light:
    the flash of love exploded and led the creation to disorder!
The detractor reason wished to know of that secret:
    but, the invisible hand of love dispatched that unwisdom!
Others cast their lot with pure pleasure:
    I sought—our loving heart chose only sweet sorrows.
My purer soul yearned for her lowly dimples, but
    my hands were led to the higher tuft of my beloved's hair.[17]
        When Hafez penned the story of the beloved's life,
        he canceled the blessed story of his own life.

Nine

Glorious! At dusk I woke with all my cares vanished:
    in that pitch black of night I drank from the water of life.
Enraptured with the glow of the inner light:
    I drank of that cup of light, glorified in nature.
What a glorious morning, what a wondrous night!
    In that mystical night, receiving a new lease in life.
Now, only my face and the face of the beloved in the mirror:
    the place where I heard the glorification of my life.
No wonder I won the prize and that rapture:
    I deserve it, these my only rewards!
The voice brought the good spell with good tidings:
    patience and integrity, rewards of my pains and suffering.
This sweetness, honey and pure sugar, my words carry:
    a reward of patience. I've tasted of that sugar and honey.
        Grace of Hafez and the breath of those night prayers
        have rescued me from slavery in pains of times.[18]

Ten

Privy to the ways of heart: you're in the garden of the beloved.
    If not, you will be in denial!
Blame me not if the ecstasy of my heart flames in public:
    thank God, it's not hidden only in my conceit!
Pseudo-Sufis[19] recovered their debts from the pawn of wine:
    unredeemed, my pawn remains in a cup.
The jailer[20] affects religion, forgetting his past,
    but my notoriety is sung in every path.
Whatever wine I drank from the crystalline hand of the beloved,
    regret was in it and changed into bitter tears.
Not Me! I carried my love from age to age in tact.
    Others! They never saw consistency in the affair.
Weary to see into the heart of the matter with discerning eyes,
    your way he could not attain, but grief in his heart.
Never heard a more delicious voice than the words of love:
    a gift lingering in the orbiting colossal dome.
That ragged garb covered my thousand flaws:
    pawned for wine and pleasure, now only the zonar bides.[21]
Perplexed, in awe of your beauteous face the painter
    leaves your face on all the walls he meets.
        Hafez lingered for a moment to savor her beauty:
        Unawares, he was caught in it for life!

Eleven

Not easy for the preacher of the city to understand:
    hypocrites and flatterers[22] cannot accept grace.[23]
Be refined in the ways of rendi, and show munificence:
    no virtue if an animal refuses wine, remaining un-evolved!
Unsullied nature alone will become worthy of grace:
    no pearl or coral will come from small pebbles.
Confident, my heart! The Almighty works his works to perfection:
    the devil cannot be tamed to become a Moslem by craft!
I make love in hopes this noble art
    will not disappoint me like any other art.
At dawn the voice kindly promised the consummation of our love:
    oh, God, keep the voice from regretting that promise.
For that beauteous face I pray for a beautiful disposition
    to keep our heart from any remorse or indisposition.
        Hafez, unless the spec of a dust rises to valor,
        how can it endure the dazzling light of our sun?

Twelve

The lover's face mirrored on the cup of wine:
    the Gnostic heard the descant, dreamed impossible thoughts.
The reflection of your beauty on the mirror
    eclipsed all the other images on the glass.
All this picture of wine and images:
    only a reflection of the visage of the cup-bearer[24] in the cup.
Distraught,[25] love sealed the tongues of his confidants,
    who dared betray publicly the secrets of his woes.
From the mosque to tavern, I fell—not my will:
    This, too, had been ordained from eternity!
No escape running in circles like a pair of compasses,
    once fallen trapped in the wheel of time.
Rescued from the well of your dimple by the strand of your hair:
    alas, delivered from the deep well, but trapped by your hair!
Never more shall I visit the cells of a monastery, my Master:
    my affair is now with the muse's face and the lip of my cup!
The sword of her sorrow hangs over my head: I dance.
    Whoever falls by her sword comes to a good end!
Each breath of hers is a blessing on me:
    Behold, if the beggar is worthy of such rewards!
        All Sufis are masters with wandering eyes, yet
        only poor Hafez has fallen into ill repute amongst them!

Thirteen

Believe me! The foundation of all desire is on shifting sand.
    Fetch the cup of wine! The story of life is written on wind!
I'm a slave to any man who, under this azured sky,
    is free of external affectations!
What can I say? Yesternight in the tavern, filled with wine,
    I heard the voice of my mystical muse, promising me wonders:
Oh, you, the regal falcon, worthy to sit on the Tree of Life[26]
    your presence in this humble place is a cause for lamentation.
You are summoned by the heavenly voices from the throne:
    I puzzle! What made you a slave to such a trap?
A word of advice: learn and act upon my words,
    a story echoing the commands of my Master.
Grieve not the pains of the world and forget not my advice:
    I've learned this, roaming the world, from a wayfarer.
Accept your fate, unknot your brows:
    you and I! We have no will in these matters.
Seek not constancy from an indifferent world, for
    this old hag is the bride of thousand suitors!
No sign of fidelity in the smile of a bud of rose:
    moan, love-mad nightingale—your cause is right!
        Why all this jealousy of Hafez, you hack-poets:
        his words and acceptance are not his, but God's.

Fourteen

The luminescence of your face pales the moon:
    compared to you, a flower becomes a weed.
The seat of my being: at the corner of your eye;
    more pleasing a place not even a king can muster!
Time will tell what becomes of the smoke of my sighs!
    A mirror suffers not readily the blowing fog!
Observe the humor: narcissus blossoms before your eyes:
    impudent eye lacks courteous gaze or glance.
I saw it all! The cruel eyes you possess
    do not favor anyone with a glance!
O Saghi, serve me a measure of your precious wine:
    the pleasure of a monk without a monastery.
Contain your heart and sit silently, for that tender heart
    has no patience with cruel noises and fight.
Tell him to leave with sorrow in his heart:
    not every person has entry to this temple.
Am I the only one to suffer her indifference?
    Show me a soul immune from her truculence.
      If Hafez worships you, there is no blame in it:
      becoming a heathen in the cause of love is no sin!

Fifteen

In our times, the only harmless friends are
    a jug of clear wine and a vessel of songs.
Go cautiously, for the passage to happiness is long and narrow:
    Take your cup, for life chances only once!
Am I the only one wearied because of ignorance?
    Our doctors? Their pall a result of the science of ignorance!
Look with sharp eyes upon this rumpus path:
    the affairs of this world are all terminal.
My heart had hoped for the consummation of our love:
    but death in the path of life is the thief of all desires.
Caress a beloved's lock of hair; quit babbling!
    Omens are in the conjunction of the heavenly stars.
        Never! Never will they find Hafez sober:
        he's drunk with the eternal wine.

Sixteen

That dark skinned lover: sweetness of honeysuckle:
    eyes, wine-soaked; lips, full of laughter; heart filled with joy.
The station of kings fills the cup with honey:
    only he has the signet of Solomon.[27]
Beautiful, versed in arts, abundant virtue:
    obviously the exemplar of both worlds is His.
That black mole, stamped on that wheaten face
    beguiled Adam out of his maze![28]
O God! The beloved is intent on leaving; oh, dear friends,
    my wounded heart! The absent beloved holds the balm!
What shall I do with my story: that hard hearted lover
    has murdered us, holding the healing breath of Jesus back.[29]
        Hafez is a believer, honor him; he's
        beheld by God's goodness and gifts.

Seventeen

Rejoice, my Saghi: it's the season of roses, tulips and verdant woods:
    let's wash the occasion thrice with your ruby wine.
Fetch the wine: I sing the ultimate beauty of the bride;
    match-maker make haste to make your match.
Sugar and honey, food for Indian parrots, like
    the sweet sound of the Persian poems in Bengal.
Distances, time lapses do not measure in songs:
    this child has paced the distance of hundred years in one.
See her bewitching eyes? Even the pious could not escape:
    her morning caravan has already started on the trail!
Be not deceived by the fraudulent beauty of the time:
    she consorts with deceit and conforms with fraud!
O West Wind, blow from the rose garden of the king:
    fill tulip's cup with the ruby wine of the dew!
        Hafez, do not neglect the audience with the Sultan:[30]
        remember, your affairs are set—by your moaning!

Eighteen

Come, Saghi: set on fire our cup of wine:
    musician––sing the news, the world has come around!
I've beheld the beauty of my love in the mirror of wine:
    O you, unaware of the perpetual pleasure of my wine!
No death invades a heart that comes alive in love:
    our immortality is etched in the book of life.
The beauty of flirtation of amorous lovers
    fades when the presence of our beloved is sensed.
O wind, if you happen upon the garden of our beloved,
    heed my words; proffer our message to our beloved.
Ask the beloved, why do you forget our name?
    It will fade in time from your memory!
I'm drunk justly by the pleasure of her gaze:
    I've submitted my lot to the wine!
Me thinks, in the Day of Judgment,
    the bread of the virtuous may fair worse than our wine!
Hafez sheds a tear or two, hoping
    the bird of union intends to come to our trap!
        The green sea of the heavens and the crescent ship
        stand in wonder at the grace of our Haji Ghavaam.[31]

Nineteen

I saw the blue[32] field of heaven and the new crescent moon:
    I thought of my own sowing and my harvest time.
I said: O fate, in your slumber the sun has reach the middle of day!
    Reply: With your kind of past, do not be disenchanted!
With angelic face and chaste—like Jesus to this universe—
    the flame of your candle casts upon the sun a hundred fold!
Never trust the thief of night; the imposter
    steals the crown of Kavoos, the golden belt of Key Khosro![33]
Gold earrings, rubies red, are heavy burden on the ear:
    the time of pleasure is running, you better heed my word!
May evil eye spare the beauty of your mole:
    in the world of beauty it eclipses the moon and that sun.
Self adulation! Do not barter your love away,
    the fields of Pleiades with a trifling grain or two!
      Flames of sham will burn the fertile fields of religion:
      Hafez, you shed this woolen sack and escape!

Twenty

Plant a tree of friendship to reap the fruits of fulfillment:
    pluck the sapling of enmity to escape pain.
When in tavern, honor the rendaan:
    else, you'll regret it when sobered.
Grasp jealously to a night's communion with friends:
    soon, days and nights will follow after our time!
O God, put in the heart of Leili's keeper of bridle
    the way of Majnoon[34] to take her cradle.
My love, seek the spring of life: in this meadow daffodils blossom
    a hundred times, nightingale sings with a thousand songs.
Haven't I signed over my love to your flowing hair?
    Fetch me the ruby wine and let it flow, as you promised!
      In this garden the ancient Hafez desires
      to sit by the flowing brook and a beauty by his side.

Twenty-One

I will never forget my beloved, who left without a word:
    with a parting word did not gladden our sorrowful heart
That fortunate youth! Caught between yes and no!
    It's a wonder he did not set free the old slave![35]
I'll wash my garment of paper[36] in blood: my fate
    did not lead me to the banner of justice.
It's a lover's hope to let you hear my voice:
    I shouted through mountains, louder than Farhad.[37]
The morning song-bird reclaimed the shadow,
    and neglected to nest in that boxwood in the meadow.
Perchance the west wind will learn from you:
    no wind has moved as gallantly as you!
The brush of the eternal beautician shall fail to paint
    the face that fails to profess your divine beauty.
O musician! Change your tune and play an Iraqi air:
    our lover so chose the path—but not a parting word!
        Hafez's hymns are Iraqi ghazals in mode:
        who heard the sad air and did not wail?

Twenty-Two

A flower blossomed from the pain of the nightingale:[38]
    the jealous wind pricked his heart with thousand thorns!
Sweet-thoughts gladdened the nightingale's heart—for a moment.
    Sudden! Flood of mortality reversed the plans of his heart!
Light of my fading eyes, fruit of my life, I remember:
    a moment of pleasure—then an incomprehensible pain!
O caravan master, my burden has fallen—O God, where is Your help?
    my hope of Your generosity! It's hid in that camel's burden!
Friend! Do not blame me: my sodden eyes, ashes on my head;
    the azured dome fashioned a pleasure home from this mud.
Dread and woes! The jealous eyes of the wheel—
    evil eyes upon my brows—made his home in the grave.
        Hafez lost occasion, the king unchecked:
        What can I say? The tricks of fate, I neglected!

Twenty-Three

Me! Just a corner of the tavern my altar:
    blessing of the beloved,[39] my morning mantra!
If I lack morning music, what of it?
    My tune is the echo of my sighs—my regrets!
Not the king nor the beggar my consort—Blessed God!
    The beggar at my beloved's door is my king!
The mosque or the tavern? Consummation is my aim:
    God is my witness! That's all I care.
Unless I fold my tent—by the sickle of death—
    it's not my style to run from my Master.
Ever since I've attended this court
    the throne of the sun has become my seat.
        Hafez, no sin is of our own willing, but
        you be polite and accept that sin!

Twenty-Four

Of late, my creed is union with beautiful faces:
    pain of this pleasure, the woes of my heart!
To see your face, inner vision is needed.
    I admit: I'm not in that league yet!
Be my beloved, for the beauty of heavens, the grace of this earth
    fades like the light of stars[40] compared to your perfection.
Since your love tutored me in the art of rhetoric,
    people praise and extol my ancient skills!
O God, bless me with the state of poverty:
    this grace, the source of my wealth and my reticence.
Preacher, will you brag you know the King's vassal?
    My heart resides in the palace with that King.[41]
O God! Who yearns to possess that vista?
    The thorns of its path, my rose and my daffodils!
        Hafez, enough of the story of Parveez!
        His lips tasted sweetness: my Khosro and my Sheereen![42]

Twenty-Five

I'm noted in the city: I'm a known lover!
    My eyes! Not set to see with a blaming gaze!
Faithful, bearing blame with ease, we are contented:
    it's profanation of our creed to be impatient![43]
I asked my Master to know the secret for salvation:
    He asked for a cup of wine and said, "Forgiveness of flaws!"
"The meaning of living in this vast garden of life:
    plucking flowers from your smile with eyes!"
"My drinking, my wine, a purpose in life,
    to destroy the demon of self-indulgence!"[44]
"So assured am I of your graceful lock of hair,
    if no resistance, what avails resisting?"
"Straight to the tavern we gallop from this gathering:
    the haranguing of the ignorant deserves escaping!"
Learning to love from the words of the beloved with open face,
    a blessing: indulge those with open faces.
        Hafez—kiss not but the lips of Saghi and the cup:
        a mistake to kiss the hand of pseudo-ascetics.

Twenty-Six

It's already morning, O Saghi, a cup full of wine: will you?
    The revolution of the wheel does not cease—do hurry!
Before the mortal world is shaken to its roots,
    shake us with a draught of rose-colored wine.
Hearken! The sun of wine rises from the east!
    If intent on pleasure, forsake your sleep!
Fate will fashion jugs from the mud of our heads;
    now fill the cup of our heads with a measure of wine!
I'm not given to idle talk, pretense to piety—or penitence:
    greet us with that clear wine in that earthen cup!
        The way of piety is in the praise of wine, Hafez.
        Rise now, resolved to serve piety!

Twenty-Seven

I spread my ashes on the path of her feet: she skirts me!
    I plead, "Turn your heart to me." She turns away!
That delicate face, she exhibits her face like a flower:
    I beg, "Open your tunic!" She covers her tunic tight.
I told my eyes, "Behold her to satisfy my hunger."
    "Will you have a stream of blood from our wells?" They cried.
She thirsts for my blood; I, her lips—we shall see!
    She'll indulge me—or, I'll have to indulge my judge!
If I'm another Farhad,[45] I've no fear of death;
    They will tell sweet stories after my life.
If my candle burns out, she will smile at my death!
    If I express my hurt, she'll be indignant at my expression!
Friends, observe: I would gladly exchange my life for one kiss;
    Such a trifle! She withholds even that from me!
        Patience, Hafez—a lesson in sorrow this might be:
        love sings in every corner a new story of me.

Twenty-Eight

I swear by the life of my Master and his blessing;
　　I bear no desire but the duty to serve my Master!
Paradise is not a place for sinners;
　　fetch that wine: I'm well aware of His mercy.
May the light of that heavenly star burn forever,
　　that set aflame the collect of the love of His presence.
If you see a head at the threshold of the tavern,
　　do not kick it, for His intent remains a mystery!
Come, my friend, filled with wine, the angel of secret
　　promises: the bounty of His mercy is ubiquitous!
Avert your contemptuous eyes from the drunken me!
　　No sin or virtue is without His decree!
I've no appetite for false virtues or contrition:
　　I'll strive in the name of Khajeh[46]—the splendor of his fortune.
　　　Hafez has forever pawned his tunic for a cup!
　　　His nature fashioned from the floor-mud of the tavern?

Twenty-Nine

Beauty of your hair puts the fragrant violet to shame:
    your delicious smile: no rose bud hopes to gain!
O scented rose, will you set on fire our nightingale?
    Who sings your praise all night—the lover's prayer!
Weary of the company of angels, yet
    I bear the chaos of the world for your sake.
What a treasure of love! Poor and proud,
    your beggar nicks the crown of kings!
The garment of virtue and the cup of wine are incompatible:
    all my plans lead to satisfy you!
The passion of the wine of your love stops my breath short:
    may this fevered head become the dust of your road.
The crown of my fancy is the seat of your vision.
    A prayer: may there never be a place without you in that place!
      Your face, a garden, especially in the spring of beauty:
      Hafez pens sweet words, serving as your bird of songs!

Thirty

In midst of flowers, a cup of wine in hand, and the lover conquered:
    they make the sovereign of the world a slave of such a day!
No need of candles tonight in this gathering:
    the full moon of the beloved's face lights our way.
In our religion wine is freely allowed, but
    without you, my beloved, the world is banned![47]
My ears to the music of that reed and the air of that harp;
    my eyes to those ruby lips and the turn of the cup of wine.
No need of perfumes in this gathering—
    the fragrance of your tresses will suffice!
No praise of the sweetness of sugar appropriate
    the day you gifted the sweetness of your lips!
The riches of your sorrow rest in my besotted heart;
    forever my residence is in the tavern's side.
No talk of disgrace—my name is shame!
    No talk of names—I'm shamed by my name!
Wined and bewildered, we were rends with roaming eyes:
    Is there anyone unlike us in this town?
And the judge![48] How can you blame him?
    He is, like us, in pursuit of—perpetual bliss!
      Hafez, do not neglect your wine and lover for long:
      time of roses, jasmine, and the Feast of Ramadan is at hand.

Thirty-One

O king of the blessed, alas loneliness!
    My heart aches for your presence—time to come back!
The flowers of this garden will soon fade away:
    help the powerless—when you have the power, my love.
Yesternight I was complaining to the wind of the beloved:
    "You're mistaken," the wind replied. "Forget this absurd notion."
Morning breeze touches her hair to dance:
    this is the rival, my heart; beware of idle acts.
My passion and your absence have led me to ask,
    how long will my patience last?
O God, who will hear my complaint on the matter?
    That ubiquitous lover shows no face to another!
Saghi, your absence pales colors in a carpet of flowers.
    Come! Saunter through green boxwoods: adorn our garden.
O what remedy for my pain—the bed of my discontent!
    My company: memory of your face, in my loneliness!
In the circle of Fortune, we're the point of yielding:
    a grace, what you think; a favor, what you order!
Freedom of will! Unknown in the kingdom of rendaan:
    abhorrent in this religion, conceit and willfulness!
Bloodied by this enameled arch, cure us with wine
    to resolve this enigma in that enameled cup!
        Hafez! Separation is done, embracing at hand:
        you mad lover, grace of happiness is coming your way!

Thirty-Two

From his solitude, the ascetic hastened to his tavern at dawn:
    forsook his promises and again took up with wine.
The Sufi of our gathering, who shattered wine cups only yesterday,
    with one draught of wine, regained his wisdom, his wit.
The love of his youth came to bed in a tender dream:
    in old age he was in love and witless again.
A young muse passing by—heart's thief and chastity!
    Pursuing that one muse—estranged from the rest!
A fiery face of rose flamed the nightingale's dwelling:
    the smiling face of candle, butterfly's scourge!
Gracious God, tears of morn—or nights—are not wasted:
    the drops of our rain water become precious pearls![49]
The eyes of Saghi sang of the miracle of enchantment:
    the circle of our prayer completing that myth.
        The home of Hafez now is a regal court:
        heart to the beloved went, life to the lover!

Thirty-Three

The light of God I see in the tavern:
    what a wonder: that light in such a place!
Do not boast of virtues, you leader of the pilgrims to Mecca!
    You only see a house, I the house of God!
I hunger to unravel those beauties' tresses for musk:
    alas, that impossible thought, reason for my mistake.[50]
Aching heart, flowing tears, sigh of the morning, moan of night
    I see all from the favor of your grace.
On my dream canvas I paint many pictures of you:
    whom can I tell what marvels I see on that canvas?
None enjoys the musk of Khotan[51] and China as much
    as I do from the scent of the morning breeze.
        Friends! Do not blame Hafez for his roaming eyes:
        I see him as a devoted lover of yours.

Thirty-Four

O Saghi, deliver the cup to reach my lips:
    love seemed easy at first; what difficulties ensued!
For the scent of musk the morning breeze gleaned from her tresses,
    how many hearts broke, awaiting that miracle?
No surety for pleasure in the place of the lover:
    the camel bells constantly call for the caravan to set!
Color your prayer rug with the red of wine—if the Master calls!
    A disciple must heed the rules of obedience!
Moonless night, fear of waves, horrid whirlwinds:
    how could they know our lot—those landlubbers!
From selfishness to infamy: I have reached my apex;
    no secret is hidden when it's spoken in public!
      If desiring His presence, do not absent yourself, Hafez:
      when you reach the lover, nothing matters in this world!

Thirty-Five

The hue of youth hovers on the garden of roses:
    sweet message reaches the honey-throated nightingale.[52]
O Morning Breeze—if you come upon the meadow-youth,
    give our regards to those roses, juniper, and the sweet basil.
If favored by the muse—that wine seller boy—
    my eyelashes will sweep the door-way of the cellar.
You twist your perfumed locks into a polo bat:
    mercy: I'm a wandering ball, scared of your polo bat!
I fear this lot, who laugh at us, the lees drinkers,
    will lose their virtues on the way to our tavern!
Follow the men of God—in Noah's ship
    there is a clump of dust, unafraid of the flood![53]
Escape to the door from the house of creation—ask not for food:
    the poison of jealousy on this plate will murder the guest!
Only a handful of dust, our final bed:
    Wonders! What need to build a Tower of Babel?
My Canaanite star, Egypt is your throne:
    Time to bid adieu—to your prison.[54]
        Hafez: drink your wine, be a rend, and live happily, but
        make not the Koran a trap of duplicity, like the others.

Thirty-Six

Friends! Let down the hair of the beloved;
    it's a wondrous night—let the tale run longer!
A private gathering, all the friends present:
    bolt the doors—recite the Koran and cover evil eyes.[55]
Rebeck and harp cry out ominously:
    heed the message of the people of secrets.
I promise, friend. Curtain of sorrow will remain distant,
    if you trust the grace of the Creator!
Much distinction between the lover and the beloved:
    if the beloved is shy, you declare your needs to her.
The foremost assertion of the Master is this word,
    "Avoid the company of the malicious minds!"
He who is not revived in our circle because of love
    I decree: perform the dead man's service while he is alive!
        If any demand a reward from you, Hafez,
        refer him to the lips of the beloved for that!

Thirty-Seven

I want bitter wine, worthy of virile strength,
    to rest for a moment from the snarls of life.
The table set by this petty life lacks sweetness or comfort:
    only a taste of greed and lust from bitterness and concern!
Fetch wine, no respite from the tricks of fate while
    Venus plays the harp, and Mars declares war![56]
Drop that hunting bow of Bahraam;[57] take up a cup of wine;
    I've trekked the plain: now no sign of Bahraam or his onagers.
Come! Let me show the secrets of the times from your clear wine,
    but you cannot show it to the ill natured—the blind of heart.
Looking upon a dervish with favor is no sign of grandeur:
    Solomon looked with favor upon a humble ant.[58]
        The bow of the brows of my beloved defies not Hafez:
        it only laughs at the lack of strength in his arms!

Thirty-Eight

The morning breeze,[59] broken and ill at ease, twisted into
    the tresses of the beloved, each break a new life for the breeze.
Where is a companion to whom I could tell
    the woes of my heartbreaks—the absence of the beloved?
The hand of creation fashioned your image from the petal of roses:
    shamefully failing, hid the image inside the yet un-opened blossoms.
You're asleep, and love cannot see a shore in sight!
    Praise be God! This road has no end.
Perhaps, the beauty of Kaaba[60] redresses the woes of those pilgrims:
    although the desert sun burns the body of those traveling in sand.
Who will bring to this broken house of woes[61]
    a sign of Joseph[62] from the well of his foes!
        I'll take that head of hair: deliver it to the judge's hands.
        Hafez is pained by that deceit and his hands!

Thirty-Nine

As you drink wine, spill a draught on the ground:
    it's no crime to benefit another soul!
Come! Consume all you have, only do not regret!
    Fate strikes its lethal sword without much regret!
I swear by the earth under your feet, my pampered beloved:
    on the day of my passing, I'll not move my feet from this earth!
What hell, what paradise, what man, what angels?
    In all religions avarice is the chief of sins.
The Architect of the universe has the six-way directions
    so firmly plugged—there is no escaping the grave.[63]
The spell of the daughter of grape is the thief of reason, but I hope
    in the day of resurrection the arbor of grapes remains in tact.
        On the way to the tavern you left this world, Hafez, welcome:
        may the prayers of the lovers go with the pure of heart.

Forty

I am not a rend to abandon my beloved—or the cup!
　　The judge knows I'm rarely guilty of such.
I've faulted many penitents often for their acts:
　　I must be insane to repent from wine at the time of roses.
Love is a pearl; I, the diver; the sea, the tavern:
　　I dove in there—where will I come up for air?
The tulip in the cup, the beloved drunk, and I called a fornicator.
　　O God, I'm in need of a judgment—who can I call for this task?
Rein in your steed for a moment, my lovely Turk, menace of peace:
　　I'll pave your way with gold and silver by my tears!
Treasures I possess, made of tears: rubies and garnets clear
　　how can I look upon the bounty of the sun in the sky?[64]
When Zephyr gracefully bathes the tuft of flowers
　　I'll be damned if I'm found to open a page of any book!
No trusting the covenant with Fortune—nor her promises;
　　I rather make a pact with the cup and wager with its bearer!
I hold in my possession the royal treasures of a beggar:
　　I cannot hunger for what this ignoble world offers!
Although wrapped in the dust of poverty—shame on me
　　if I wet my shirt in the fountain of the sun!
If the pleasure of the Friend is to see the lovers in the fire,
　　my coveting gaze will fix upon the River Kosar.[65]
　　　　Yesternight your ruby lips flirted with Hafez,
　　　　but I'm not the one to believe in such fables!

Forty-One

The king of beauties, sovereign of sweet hearts,[66]
    heart breaker of the brave with the sharpness of her eyes,
Filled with wine, passing by, took a look at me, a poor dervish,
    and said, "You, beloved of all the sweet word-smiths,
How long will you sit with your purse empty of gold and silver?
    Be my slave![67] Indulge in all the delights of those beauties!
No less than a speck of dust you are, aim high—make love
    to rise to the private mansion of the Sun[68] while dancing!
If a cup of wine in hand, trust this cosmos not;
    savor the beauty of the sisters of Venus—the slender ones."
My Master—a lover of the cup—may his soul rest in peace, once
    said, "Shun the company of those who break their promise.[69]
Hold to your friends; dissolve your connection with enemies.
    Be of God's grace; leave Ahriman to his devices."
I was asking the breeze this morning in a field of red tulips:
    "Whose martyrs lie in the field with blood soaked shrouds?
        Hafez said, "To that secret—you and I are not privy:
        Just talk of the ruby wine—and those beauties!"

Forty-Two

What is more pleasing than the thought of wine and a cup
  to glean what ultimately will happen!
How long shall I sorrow: the time is fleeing?
  Be kind hearted: what of the passing of time?
Tell the impatient bird to sorrow for itself—
  what mercy the hunter shows when setting his traps?
Drink wine, avoid all sorrows—do not listen to bogus advice:
  what truth flows from common advice?
Your wages better spent on your service to pleasure:
  you know the dues owed the misers of life!
Yesternight my Master was reciting the riddle
  inscribed on the wine, foretelling our union.
      I've stolen Hafez's heart with harp, tambourine, and songs:
      we'll see what punishment the infamous me will have!

Forty-Three

That clear, blood-red gem, my beloved's thirsty lips:
    in the pursuit of seeing it, giving my soul the task.
Pity her black eyes and long lashes:
    anyone to see her flirtations—my denial.
Cameleer, do not lead to the gates; that way
    lies the highway to the home of my beloved.
I'm a slave of my lucky star, for in the absence of fate
    the love of that tippled vagabond is my lot.
A drum of the rose oil, her hair scattering perfume is
    a grace sample of the scent from the perfumer.
Gardner, do not deny your doors to Zephyr:
    the water of your garden is from the tears of my love.
Sugar water, rose sherbet from the lips of my love:
    the healer of my heart is her delicious eyes.
        Any who taught Hafez the point of the ghazal
        is the sweet-tongued friend of his witty words.

Forty-Four

O God—sit not with those sack-clad pious pretenders:
  nor hide your face from those wandering rendaan.[70]
The woolen sacks: abundant dirt they hide;
  welcome is a simple wine-seller's robe.
These pseudo Sufis: no clear consolations they give;
  may the wine of the lees[71] drinkers change to clear wine.
Your sensitive nature cannot bear to wear
  the burden of those sack-robed pretenders.
I'm spoiled by that wine; hide not your face.
  After the sweet nectar, feed me no poison.
Come and observe the fraud of these impostors:
  our cup, filling with blood, our lute playing in discord!
    Beware of the hopeful warmth Hafez exudes:
    his heart is in a turmoil, a boiling pot.

Forty-Five

Me! Refusing a cup of wine? What a fable:
　　my head is working—sometimes—sufficiently!
Not knowing my path—towards the tavern's direction—
　　was the cause of my reluctant sobriety.
The pious with conceit and prayer, I, sauced and in despair:
　　till you grant your favor—to whomever you wish!
The pious do not follow the path of rendaan: granted,
　　but love is of an essence, above any circumspection!
A foe of piety, reveling nightly with the tambourine and harp,
　　if I renounce my old habits, so what is this discussion?
I'm slave to my Tavern-Master, who freed me from my innocence:
　　whatever he did, it was the pure soul of reverence.
　　　　Last night grief forbade sleep, for a friend decreed:
　　　　"If Hafez is drunk, I'm despairing, indeed."

Forty-Six

Even a moment's grief—the world is not worth it;
    I'll sell my robe for a cup of wine: that's all it's worth it.
The wine merchant in the alley will not trade
    my prayer-rug for a cup of wine; it is not worth even that.
"Forget this matter," blamed my Master,[72] my ragheeb:
    "our woes, merely a scrap of dust; it isn't worth it.
The glory of a crown, inscribed with the news of harm:
    what a wondrous hat, but losing the head? It is not worth it."
So easy the voyage seemed: what abundant gains!
    I was wrong: then came the storm! For diadems, it wasn't worth it!
Best to cover your face, away from your admirers: it is the joy
    of the conquest of armies, but sorrow pursues; it isn't worth it.
        Like Hafez, seek prudence and pass by this inferior orbit:
        a grain of false favor for a ton of silver; it isn't worth it.

Forty-Seven

A nightingale once carried a petal of rose in her beak:
  her ravishing song and the petal, yet she moaned in grief.
I said, "Your lover is present! Why this moaning and sorrow?"
  She replied, "It's the presence of the lover!"
If the beloved sit not with us—no matter:
  a haughty ruler, she is weary of a beggar.
Our prayers, our love does not sit well with our lover.
  Happy the man who has luck with his beauties.[73]
Rise! Let's offer our lives to the brush of that Architect,[74] who
  has framed so many designs in the motion of a pair of compasses.
If a disciple of the path of love, fear not infamy:
  Sheikh Sanaan[75] pawned his garment for wine.
How fortunate, that galandar[76] in his journeys
  wore zonar,[77] yet kept the prayer rosary[78] in his hand.
    Eyes of Hafez gaze at the palace of his lover
    like "Streams flowing in a garden from its slopes."[79]

Forty-Eight

Precious time, value it high:
>   fruit of life, this moment is understanding.
The cycle of life offers bounty—expecting a return:
>   try to receive your bonus in pleasure.
O gardener, when I pass from this place—may you live in hell[80]
>   if you plant in my place an unfriendly juniper.
A remorseful ascetic will die of his passion for wine:
>   wisdom dictates we avoid deeds requiring regrets!
Ah! The jailer is unaware that our Sufi
>   stashes his home-made wine—like ruby-red tears!
Do not quarrel with those who pray for you:
>   it's in the spell of one single name, the signet of Solomon.[81]
Heed the advice of the lovers: come to the door of pleasure:
>   it's not worth the price—this passing cycle!
Dear Joseph has disappeared: mercy brothers!
>   Terrible! I see in deep sorrow the ancient of Canaan![82]
Caution: never talk of rendi in front of an ascetic:
>   you cannot tell an unknown healer of your secret pain.
You run away: the memory of your eye-lashes spills my blood;
>   you run too fast, my love! Me thinks you'll stall!
I had kept the arrows[83] of your eyes in my heart, but
>   the bow of your brow shamelessly mocks.
Befriend the afflicted Hafez with tenderness:
>   the breaks of your tresses, the source of his distresses.
>   If you're finished with me, you cruel beloved,
>   I'll complain my station with the second vizier.[84]

Forty-Nine

Oh, Wind, kindly tell that tender gazelle;
    you've exiled us—crazed—to wilderness and hills.
The sugar merchant—may he live long—
    would he not remember that sugar-craving parrot?
Did the vanity of your beauty forbid—oh, rose—
    your asking after the love-sick nightingale?
The wise will hunt with humor and kindness;
    traps and harnesses will not hold the gifted bird.
I know not why there is no sign of recognition
    from that tall, black-eyed beauty's face.
When you sit with your beloved to drink a draught,
    remember those absent, whom you toasted once!
Nothing more need be said about your faults:
    faith and charity are absent from your beautiful face.
        No wonder in heaven—Hafez says—
        The song of Venus brings dance to the Messiah.

Fifty

Oh! If that Shirazi Turk steal my heart
    I'll gift to her Indian Mole, both Samrakand and Bokhara.
Pour the remaining wine, Saghi![85] —in paradise you shall not find
    the river banks so firm—nor the soft pleasure of a prayer rug.
Behold these brazen beauties, menace to the peace of town:
    they stole patience from my heart, like Turkish Khans in plunder.
The face of the beloved is pleased with our unconsummated love:
    what need a beauteous face has of earth, water, or art?
From the ever-increasing beauty of Joseph, this I understood:
    love rends the curtain of virtue from Zoleykha's[86] face.
If you curse—if you abuse me, I'll pray for you:
    bitter response suits the ruby lips of the sweetest heart.
Heed my words, my love: more precious than life
    the lucky youth holds the advice of the virtuous sage.
Come, sing of wine and minstrels—seek less the secrets of life;
    none has solved—nor can—this enigma with the logic of mind.
      Hafez, you sang ghazal,[87] made pearls of words; come and sing:
    the Universe graces your verse with a marriage to the Pleiades.

Fifty-One

Where do I stand—the wretched—and where discretion?
   The enormous gap: from where to where!
Bored with a hermit's life—in an impostor's garb—*you* tell me:
   where is that tavern of the magicians, where the cleared wine?
What connects a libertine with virtue—and, discretion?
   Where are the sermons, where the sound of a viol?
What discerns an enemy from the face of a friend?
   Where is the dead lamp, where the luminance of the sun?
The cure for my insight is from the dust of your door—
   where shall we go, tell me, from this self to where?
Do not slip by the dimple of the chin; the well is yet on our way;
   where are you rushing, my love, why such haste, where?
Oh that the consummation of love were sweetly remembered;
   where did all your flirtation go, where that reproach in your eyes?
      Expect not from Hafez sleep or rest, dear friend.
      What is patience? Where is rest—where, sleep?

Fifty-Two

From mosque to tavern sauntered our Master—yesternight;
    what is, my fellow pilgrims, our path?
We, the disciples, turn towards Mecca—
    our Master moves toward the vintner's shop.
In the tavern of the virtuous faith, we become companions:
    so our fate ordained from eternity.
If the mind knew the heart were happy with love's ties,
    the wise would feign madness in pursuit of our chains.
To us, the goodness of your face kindly reveals the secret:
    nothing in our mind, but goodness and kindness.
Your heavy heart—does it kindle on a night
    with our fiery sighs, your heart aflame—only a night's affair?
        Silence, Hafez! The arrows of our sighs go through the body of Fate;
        take heed for your life: avoid the sting of that arrowhead!

Fifty-Three

Tousled hair, sweating, a smile on her lips—drunk!
    Slashed-shirt, a song on her lips, a cup in her hand.
The flower of her eyes, an argument; her lips filled with regret:
    yesternight she came to my bed—and sat!
She brought her lips to my ear and sang—melancholic voice—
    "Oh, my inveterate lover: are you asleep?"
"Given to such a nocturnal wine, a lover,
    if not a drunk, the lover's traitor be!"
Go, you virtuous hermit—find no fault with those in pain:
    the only gift we received from eternity.
Whatever He poured into our cup, we drank:
    if heavenly nectar—if intoxicating wine!
        Oh, the laughter of that wine cup —the curly hair of the beloved:
        how much contrition, broken like the repentance of Hafez!

Fifty-Four

Of late, my faith is peddling with the idols:
>   this sorrow, the happiness of my mournful heart.
A glimpse of your face must be the vision of life:
>   this, hardly the level of my vision of the creation.
Be my love, for the beauty of the Firmament and the grace of Time—
>   the mist on your face and your tears—are my guiding light.
Since your love inspired me to sing my song,
>   the word in the bazaar sings my praise.
Oh, Lord, bestow on me the wealth of poverty:
>   this grace is my deign, my humility.
You, divines, you Pharisees, no more words of splendor:
>   the habitat of the Sultan, my desolate heart.
O God, whose spectacle is this ultimate goal:
>   the thorns of its path, my flowers and roses?
>   Hafez, do not sing of the discretion of Parviz—ever:
>   his lips, like Khosro and Sheereen's, the cup of my lips.

Fifty-Five

Come, Sufi, see the clear mirror in the cup:
    behold the purity of the red ruby in the wine.
Oh! The besotted libertine knows the secrets
    behind the veil, hidden from the virtuous ascetic men!
Remove your traps! Phoenix cannot be caught:
    will you hold the snare in vain till the doomsday comes?
At the banquet of Time, drink a cup—or two—then leave;
    that is: you cannot covet eternal bliss.
Our youth fled, O Heart, before you could pick a flower of pleasures;
    Then, O Spirit, my guide—do not talk of our fame or shame.
Delight yourself with the pleasures at hand:
    draught availed not Adam in Paradise.
Much debt of duty we owe at your feet, O Master:
    look down upon me, your slave, with indulgence.
        O West Wind, Hafez is devoted to his jaam of wine:
        Reach Sheikh Jaam with our word of obedience!

Fifty-Six

It's not she—flowing hair, beauteous body—the beloved:
    I'm the slave of the one with that other Beauty!
Oh, the beauty of the nymphs and fairies, elegant and fair,
    but the real elegance—the grace—has the other virtue!
You, laughing rose, behold the fountain of mine eyes:
    it's only that hope, gracing my soul.
The sun above—the delight of its orbit—
    is not a rider, reins in hand!
My words—soon you accepted—were accepted:
    Oh, yes! Yes, the word of love has its own tokens.
The bow of your brow—in the art of archery—
    has triumphed over those with a bow at hand.
In the path of love, none is privy to the secret—not for surety:
    each suspicion, each according to his wits.
With the denizens of the tavern, munificence of wine,
    for every word has its own time, and every point its spot.
The clever bird, she sings not her tune in the meadow:
    she knows—each Spring eventually is followed by its Fall.
      You, critics! You cannot sell riddles to Hafez—nor epigrams!
      Our pen has its own luminous tongue, its own expression.

Fifty-Seven

Come, you! Come launch our ship in a river of wine:
    incite with joyous shouts—the old and young!
Come! Cast me—O my muse—in a ship of wine,
    for it is said: do good, then throw it in the rushing waters.
I've repented from the path of the tavern, the sinful way;
    in your kindness, point me to the pious path.
Bring me a cup of that rosy wine—the scent of musk:
    ignite jealousy, envy, in the heart of the scented rose-water!
Granted! I'm a reprobate drunk: look upon me kindly so;
    look gently upon this broken heart of mine.
If desiring the sun at mid-night, then remove
    the cover off the face of that beauteous daughter of vine.
When the day comes, the day of my burial,
    take me to the tavern; cast me into that vat of wine!
      When the world is too much with you, O Hafez,
      hurl the arrow of a shooting star at the demon of the sorrows!

Fifty-Eight

Arise! Fill the golden cup—with joyous tidings
    before the cup of my head becomes a dirt scoop!
The end—our perpetual home—is the valley of silence:
    now echo joyous songs from the heaven's dome!
Tainted look! No, it's absent from a lover's face:
    cast your eyes like the unsullied reflection from a mirror.
O Green Juniper, when I'm buried in the dust of your feet,
    deny your coyness, cast your shadow upon my dust.
My heart poisoned by the snake of your hair;
    now heal my wound with the antidote of your lips.
Accept: the possessions of this meadow have no surety:
    set aflame from the heart of wine these possessions.
I'm baptized by the tears of my eyes, for the wise declare:
    first be cleansed, then cast your eyes upon the virtuous one.
That conceited hermit, O God, who never saw but blemish,
    channel his darkness into the mirror of understanding!
        For her breath, like a rose, shed your garment, Hafez:
        Then spread this wrap on your nimble lover's path!

Fifty-Nine

Do not grieve: Joseph, lost, he returns to Canaan;
    the hut of sorrow turns to a rose garden—do not grieve.
This heart, mournful, it will heal, do not despair;
    this head, frenzied, it will heal—do not grieve.
Perchance, Heaven denies our desires for a day—or two:
    there is no constancy to the motion of time—do not grieve!
If the spring of life climbs the green throne of the meadow,
    you, the song bird, again will dance with that rose—do not grieve.
Despair! Who is privy to mysteries of the invisible?
    Behind the curtain, such hidden games—do not grieve!
When the rushing flood of doom slashes your life,
    Noah is your captain in this gale—do not grieve.
In the barren desert if treading in the delight of Kaaba and
    the thorn bushes suture your feet in blame—do not grieve.
Oh, the home is fraught in danger, destination void,
    but there is not a single path—sans end—do not grieve!
Separation from the beloved, importuning of the rival,
    all known to our God—do not grieve.
        Hafez, in the depths of poverty and the void of dark nights,
        your benediction and lessons come from the Koran—do not grieve.

Sixty

I lose my heart, the virtuous, his God.
    Alas, the night's secrets will show in the day light.
We are the ship-wrecked: oh, rise merciful wind.
    Perchance, again I may see the lover's familiar face.
The ten days of the wheel,[88] filled with tales and charm,
    be generous to friends, appreciate your loves.
In the feast of flower and wine, thus sang the nightingale at dawn:
    "O Saghi, bring the jug of wine; awake, you, besotted men!"
Oh, you generous man, grateful for your health;
    show kindness to a poor beggar man.
The peace of the world impinges on two simple phrases:
    generosity with friends—prudence with enemies.
We are not given access to the path of reputation:
    if you don't like it so—try changing your fate!
That virulent liquid![89] "Mother of all evil," the Sufi call:
    God will reject the prayer of him who imbibes from that wine.
When in poverty, seek pleasure in wine:
    this alchemy of soul, makes a beggar, Gharoon![90]
Refractory! Don't be like a candle from zeal, you'll burn
    your love, in whose hands wax feels wax a stone.
Alexander's mirror is a goblet of wine[91]—observe it well:
    May it offer you the kingdom of Daaraa.[92]
If the minstrels of the rivals sing my Persian words,
    those virtuous sages will be seduced to rapture![93]
        Do not wear, Hafez, your wine-soaked garments:
        absolve us of all this, you virtuous preachers!

Sixty-One

For long, our heart has yearned to possess Jamsheed's Cup,
    begging for what it already possesses,
Like a pearl, floating out of its cosmic shell,
    begging for help from those, themselves lost on the sea shore.
Yesternight, I took my question to the wise Magus,
    by all accounts the arbiter of resolutions.
I saw him! Cheerful, full of laughter, a cup of wine in hand,
    scanning that ruby mirror with his eyes—a hundred times!
I asked, "Oh, sage, who gifted you this cup of perceptions—when?"
    He replied, "When this azured Dome, He was fashioning last."
"God walked with a blind man under all conditions;
    failing to recognize Him, the man cried, 'Oh, where are you, God?'
See! That friend, whose head adorns that gallows pole:
    he sinned! Yes, he revealed hidden secrets!
If the Holy Spirit once again intervenes,
    many might do what the Messiah did."
        I asked, "Those ringlets on the idols' curls—for what purpose?"
        He replied, "Oh, Hafez is just bemoaning his love-sick heart!"

Sixty-Two

To the tavern, once again—if breath is left in me:
    the service of the libertines—no other task for me.
Happy the day I saunter—teary eyed—
    to knock at the tavern doors—again.
Lack of insight in this community—help me, O God:
    I'll carry my pearls to another nation.
A friend leaves—does not honor our old affections—
    no matter, God forbid: I'll pursue another comrade.
Should the circle of this azured wheel prove favorable,
    with my other pair of compasses, I'll draw him back.
My heart yearns for health, happiness—if only
    amorous glances permit—or, another thieving hair.
Oh, look at our hidden secrets—shouted publicly
    with pipes and tambourines in other market places.
My heart aches: the firmament hourly
    intends to tend my wounded heart with another hurt.
        Again I say nay—Hafez is no exception:
        in this wilderness many others have been lost!

Sixty-Three

The hidden secrets the Gnostic knew from the glow of wine.
    Only from that glow you know a mortal's mettle.
Who but the morning bird knows the price of the garden rose?
    Not all who can read a page will understand its meaning.
Both worlds I offered my wounded heart:
    alas, but for your love, it deemed all perishably mortal.
I will not any more heed the gossip of the common man:
    even the sheriff has ceded to my concealed pleasures!
Alas! The beloved believes not in our tranquility:
    otherwise she would have known the pangs of our anxiety!
Stone and mud, they can turn to rubies and agates with felicity
    if they understand the divine decrees of the morning wind.
You, who learn about the miracle of love from the books of wisdom,
    I fear you will not know the point with any clarity!
Fetch my wine: he cannot boast of the spring flowers in the garden
    who knows the plundering of autumnal winds.
        This pearl in verse, incited by his poetic gift, Hafez
        considers the vestiges of the teachings of his Old Master.

Sixty-Four

Let's rise, carry openly the Sufi's cloak to the tavern:
   lay contradictions and idle talk in the market place of superstition.
Our journey brought us to the rendaane galandar.[94]
   Let us offer Bestami[95] sack-cloth as our grateful gifts.
So that all the solitary hermits share a morning draught—
   take morning music to the door of the Supplicant Master.
With you, that covenant we made in the secrets of the desert—remember?
   If not like Moses, pray tell, we will return to the appointed places.[96]
Sound the drums of Your glory to the heights of the heavens:
   raise the news of your Love to the very roofs of creation.
Tomorrow,[97] the dirt of your path to the valley of the resurrection goes—
   with much pride, we'll shower our heads with that dirt.
If the hermit lays thorns of blame on our paths,
   from the rose garden to the jail of misery we shall take him.
Shame! With my cloak defiled, with this lack of candor,
   how shall I utter the name of the eternal God?
If the heart grasps not the moment,[98] remaining idle,
   much shame will rain upon us?
Mischief rains from the high roof of skies, arise!
   Let's seek shelter from all this harm—in the tavern.
How long to be lost in the desert of this mortality?
   Let's ask the way—perhaps we'll come to the heart of cognition.[99]
      Hafez, waste not your grace on any spiteful man;
      a better purpose, yet: let's hasten to the Judge of all men.

Sixty-Five

Yesternight, I saw angels knocking at the tavern door:
    they molded Adam's mud to exact measures.[100]
The denizens of purity and angelic shame
    joined me—a beggar—in a cup of wine!
Heavens could not bear to carry—the Trust:[101]
    they stamped the task as my lot.
Forgive the wars among the seventy-two nations:
    unwilling to see the truth, they led the way to fiction.[102]
Praise God! Peace between Him and me!
    Now Sufis drink with steps of dance in gratitude!
Not the fire the flame of the candle ridicules:
    but the blaze that sets the field of moth[103] afire.
        None could unveil the face of thoughts as Hafez,
        who combed the unruly hair of words with his pen.

Sixty-Six

You, hermit—pure of heart—with rendaan find no faults:
    you will not be debited with the sins of another!
If I'm good—or, bad—you be what you are:
    you'll reap, at the end, what you have sown.
Drunk or sober, we're all seekers of the beloved:
    Mosque or Synagogue—everywhere is the house of love.
My head in surrender against the bricks of the tavern wall; if the foe
    understands not my word, tell him: "It's your head and the bricks!"
Tell me no disheartening tale of the grace of God:
    who knows, behind the curtain, who's good, who ugly?
I'm not alone to fall from the height of piety:
    my father, too, let paradise slip from his hands!
      Hafez, in the end, if you divine a cup of wine in your hand,
      they'll carry you instantly from the tavern to heaven.

Sixty-Seven

To your foes, don't reveal the secrets of love, nor drunkenness:
    let the pretender die—ignorant—in the pain of self indulgence.
Fall in love, lest one day the business of the world cease, and you
    untutored in the designs of life from the loam of Existence.
How well that idol said—yesternight—in the presence of the Magi:
    "Why question the heathen, if you're not an Idolater?"
My lord—Oh God!—your hair breaks us;
    how long will it last—all these intrusions?
In the corner of safety, how can I hide myself,
    unless your eyes divulge the mystery of drunkenness?
That day—I saw it all, when this sedition leapt:
    mutinous for a time, you refused to sit with us!
      Your love, Hafez, will deliver you to the storm:
      did you think, like the lightening, you escaped this fight?

Sixty-Eight

From the corner of the tavern, the invisible voice—yesternight
    whispered, "Drink your wine; they'll forgive your sin."
God's grace, indwelling, works well:
    the Angel of mercy brings this news.
God's grace transcends our sins;
    why this secret mumbling, then? Keep silence!
This naïve wisdom you take to the tavern,
    till the blood boils with the ruby wine.
Though the union happens not because of works,
    you try as hard as you might, my heart.
My ears kissing the ringlets of my beloved's hair;
    my face covered with the vintner's doorway dirt.
Hafez's rendi is no unforgivable sin
    with the favor of the forgiving king.
The arbiter of religion, Shah Shoja, and his command
    have the ear of the Holy Spirit with demand.
        Oh, Lord, fulfill his wishes with your grace
        and keep him safe from the perils of evil eyes.

Sixty-Nine

Head exploding with joy, I shout:
    "From the cup I seek, the flow of life."
Mellow heads cannot bear to wear the grim face of an ascetic:
    I'm a slave to the one who drinks to the lees.
Should the tavern-keeper refuse to open that door,
    which door shall I knock, from where seek my healing?
Blame me not for growing wild in this pasture:
    as I'm nurtured, I grow!
Judge me not by your monastery—nor by my tavern:
    God, my witness! Wherever He is, I am with Him.
The dust of quest breathes the alchemy of prosperity:
    I am a slave to that amber-perfumed dust.
Oh, the delight of the wine-soaked eyes of a beloved:
    like a tulip—with the cup—I yearn the taste on my lips.
        Bring that wine—Hafez has so decreed—to cleanse
        our hearts from deceit—in the grace of that cup.

Seventy

I have said it often—once again I confess:
    ravished heart, this path I seek not on my own.
Behind the mirror, I am kept like a parrot."
    Whatever the Eternal Master tells... I repeat.
If I'm a clod of thorn—a flower bud—there is the Gardner:
    from the caress of His hand, I'm made to grow.
Oh, friend, find no faults in me, a befuddled, love-sick man;
    a pearl in my hand, I seek a man of clear sight.
Coarse garment of piety and rosy wine will not mix,
    but I'll never blame then absolve him from his deceitful sins!
Lovers cry and they weep, their sources in different mansions:
    I sing at night, in the morning I weep.
        Hafez said, "Do not smell the dust of the tavern door,"
        You replied, "No blaming: I only smell the musk from China."

Seventy-One

The power who gave your face the color of roses and narcissus
    could gift to me, a beggar, patience and peace.
And he who taught your tresses the rules of aggression
    his grace could bring justice to me, a mourner.
I abandoned my hopes in Farhaad[104] the day
    he allowed the full reign of his heart to the lips of Sheereen.
If goldsmith's treasures are unavailable, thrift will do:
    whoever gave that to the kings, gave this to beggars!
A beautiful bride is this world—on the face—
    whoever makes the connection, gives his life as kabeen.[105]
From now on: my hand on the skirt of juniper—and the bank of a brook:
    happily the breeze brings the tidings of Farvardeen.[106]
      In the hand of life's woes, Hafez's heart is bloodied:
      from the absence of the face of Khajeh Ghavam Aldeen.[107]

Seventy-Two

Heavens intone, "Spring is come, green the meadows."
   If our wages come, we'll spend it on flowers and wine.
The song bird complains, "Where is the vat of wine?"
   Nightingale wails, "Who unveiled the roses?"
Can a man delight in the fruits of Paradise
   if he fails to take a bite from the apple-chin of a beauty?
Cease complaining about your woes; on the way of fulfillment,
   he will find no comfort, who has avoided suffering.
From the face of that beauteous Saghi, pick a flower this day:
   the face of the garden is blazing with violets.
Flirtations of the Saghi steal my heart such:
   I cannot hold hands with the desire of another.
I'll burn this ragged, flowery garment of mine:
   even the old wine-seller will nor exchange it for a cup!
      Spring is fading fast, oh justiciar understand!
      The season is already passed; Hafez hasn't yet tasted wine!

Seventy-Three

We will not speak ill, nor incline to injustice,
    dye our garment azure blue,[108] and others in black.
Judging the poor and rich by "less" or "more" is evil.
    It's an absolute to avoid such indiscretion.
We'll not write sophistic notes in the book of knowledge:[109]
    nor, add true secrets to the page of charlatans.
If the king drinks not the unclear wine of the rendaan with respect,
    we'll not look kindly on the pure wine of his court!
We'll ride the world joyously in the path of our soul:
    will never think of a black horse, nor a saddle of gold.
Cruel dome breaks the ship of the talented artist:
    it's best avoid trusting that dome!
If I'm vilified by a jealous enemy—and a friend is annoyed,
    tell him to rejoice: I never pay heed to an idiot!
        Hafez, if an enemy utters outlandish words, we forgive:
        if he speaks the truth, we have no fight with the man!

Seventy-Four

Forty years since I have been declaring:[110]
    the lowest of the devotees of the Master[111] I am.
By the grace of the love of the Old Vintner[112]
    my cup has never emptied of clear wine!
From the love and charity of the risk-taking rendaan
    my place has always been on the platform.[113]
In my honor do not berate the lees drinkers:
    the coat is soiled, but my hands, clean.
The royal falcon of the King I am; what folly
    to forget the flight and perch of my band.
A nightingale, I'm imprisoned in this cage;
    the words of my tongue sweet, but I'm silenced in fact.[114]
The climate of Fars[115] fosters mean folk:
    where is a companion to help fold my tent from this land?
How long will you hide under the cloak your jug, Hafez?
    In the banquet of Khajeh,[116] I'll rend your veil!
      Honor be to you, Tooran Shah, that in bidding up my price
      your many gifts have become a noose around my neck!

Seventy-Five

Those who change lead into gold[117] with a mere wink of their eyes,
    O God, would that they glance at us from the corner of their eyes.
Better my pain hidden from the counterfeit healers;
    perhaps my medicine will come from the house of hidden sources.
Since the beloved would not remove her mask:
    everyone imagines a fresh story in his mind.
Salvation comes not from rendi[118] —nor ascetic mind:
    it's better to hope, leaving your affairs to grace.[119]
Do not remain oblivious to gnosis, for in the bartering of love
    the initiate barter with intimate souls.[120]
Now, much sedition behind the curtain rules;
    with the curtain rent, what sedition rules?[121]
If granite objects to this story—no wonder!
    The wise will understand the story of a broken heart.
Toast a cup or two: a thousand sins behind a private veil
    better than worshiping in public with guile.
That shirt, soaked with Joseph's scent,
    I fear the jealous brothers will rend it.[122]
Saunter by the alley leading to the tavern once—the assembled lot
    there will spend time to pray for your soul!
Concealed from the envious, invite me to your presence:
    the charity of a patron is offered in secret—for the sake of the Lord.
        Hafez, permanent union is impossible
        from ungracious kings towards a beggar.

Seventy-Six

Sovereigns bow in your presence—slave to your wine-soaked eyes:
    The sober[123] drunk with the ruby wine of your lips!
The morning breeze[124] betrayed you—I, the tears of my eyes:
    surely lovers keep their own secrets firm!
When passing under the twain strands of her hair, look with care:
    they bemoan both the left and right!
Be the morning breeze: steal upon the melancholic violets to see
    how restive they lie from the assault of your hair.
Ours is The Garden, O Man of God—leave us:
    only sinners deserve the miracle of forgiveness.
Not I alone sing the praise of the flower of your face:
    the songs of nightingale resound in thousands from all directions.
You yield, O happy and auspicious Khezr,[125] for I—
    I walk on foot, my companions ride their steeds.
Come, my friend, to the tavern and feel the warmth of wine:
    only sinners find their way to a monastery!
        May Hafez never feel free of that flowing hair: only
        those bound to the arch of your brows are saved.

Seventy-Seven

In all the taverns, none like me can be found so enraptured!
  My coat the pawn of wine in a shop, my verse in another!
My heart, a regal mirror,[126] is burdened:
  I beg God for the company of an enlightened man.
I've repented in the hands of the ravishing wine-seller
  never to drink wine without the presence of a beauty!
If narcissus[127] boasts of her eyes, complain not, my beloved:
  the discerning heart will not seek the eyes that have no sight.
Perchance, the candle will tell its story, for
  the butterfly lacks any interest in telling that story.[128]
I've launched rivers of tears from my eyes
  in hopes a beauty[129] will sit by my side.
Fetch my ship, my cup of wine; I grieve for my lover's absence:
  each corner of my eyes, an ocean—the fruit of my woes.
Not another word with me, the lover!
  No care have I, but wine and my beloved!
What a delicious story the Christian told this morning
  at the door to the tavern, playing his tambourine and reed:
    The way Hafez practices his Islam,
    woe if today is followed by a tomorrow![130]

Fasting month gone, the feast at hand, hearts, in sheer excitement:
    the wine is full aged in the tavern—we must run to drink it.
The time of the merchants of false virtue is over:
    it's the turn of the rendaan—to revel!
Blame the wine drinker? What a fractious fiction?
    What a mistake, what an untenable imputation!
Drinking wine with a pure heart, free of falsity,
    is more desirable than peddling virtue with falsity.
We are not sophistic rendaan—nor an opponent of dissension:
    The Holder of Secrets is our witness.
We give Him God's due—hold no malice for any one;
    whatever lawful, we do not abrogate.
What happens if you and I drink a cup—or two?
    Wine is the blood of grape-vine, not yours!
        What is this fault, perjuring all other faults?
        If so—show those innocent folk!

Seventy-Nine

O Morning breeze, tell me! Where my beloved lives?
  The dwelling of that deadly, furtive beauty!
Dark night, the secure path in the desert up front,
  where is the fire on the Mountain,[131] when the encounter?
Born to this world? The end is death:
  ask in the tavern, "Where is the sober one?"
Only the initiate will know of the intimations.
  Much remains hidden; where is the keeper of hidden secrets?
Each hair of my head has thousands of questions to ask.
  Where am I, and where is the idle blamer?[132]
Again, you ask the breaks of my lover's tresses,
  "This mournful, addled heart of mine, whence imprisoned?"
My sapience went mad:[133] where are the jet black tresses?
  Our heart hinted: where is the brow of our beloved?
The cup bearer, musician, and wine, all prepared:
  pleasure sans a lover is impossible, where is my beloved?
      No woes—the autumnal wind blowing over time's meadow.
      Hafez, be honest: where is a thornless flower?

Eighty

My breast aflame from the fevered heart: languishing for the lover.
  Such flames in this house will burn the works.
My body melts for the absence of the lover;
  my soul afire for a glimpse of the face of my beloved.
How intense the pain of my heart, the candle at dawn
  burned like a moth in love with the fire.
A friend—not a stranger—is always sympathetic;
  seeing my pain, even the stranger became empathic!
The brook from the tavern washed away my virtue;
  the flames of the tavern burned away my reason.
Repentance shattered my heart, like a glass goblet of wine;
  like a candle, my heart flamed—for wine and the tavern.
Make haste, come again: I see in my eye's mirror
  my cloak rent away, burning with grace![134]
    Leave the fables, Hafez, and drink a draught:
    we remain awake all night, the candle burning with our tale!

Eighty-One

My lover came to me in the tavern, a cup of wine in hand;
  sopped with wine—drinkers drunk from her besotted eyes.
In the shoe of her horse, I see the face of the new moon emerge;
  compared to her tall figure, juniper seemed lowly and wanting.
What can I confirm? I cannot confirm my self!
  How can I deny my beloved, while my gaze is glued on her?
The candle of my loving heart quenched, as she rose:
  when she sat, voyeurs bemoaned her act.
Musk is perfumed because my beloved has used it;
  woad colors her brows: my beloved uses that![135]
    Return to me so that the spent life returns to Hafez:
    the arrow once shot from the bow will never return.

Eighty-Two

The gaze of my eyes,[136] your nesting domicile:
    kindly descend and perch; the house is your mansion!
The grace of your plumage has stolen the Sufi's[137] heart:
    wondrous secrets hide under your seed and your trap.
May your union with the flower, O nightingale, be auspicious:
    in the meadow all songs are your warbling for love.
To heal our fragile heart, point us to your lips:
    this exhilarating ruby[138] is hid among your treasures.
Confined in body, the gift of your diligence,
    but in truth, my body the dust of your path.
Not given to offering my heart to any beauty:
    the doors of this treasure-house bear your seal and amity.
What a beauty you are, O you graceful master equestrienne:
    your whip has tamed the wild steed of this cosmos.
Not my place to sleight the magician's universe
    with the deceit that is in the bag of your sorcery.
        The hymn of our audience—anon the universe will dance:
        it's the poem of Hafez, the sweet singer, which is your song!

Eighty-Three

The preacher makes a show on the pulpit,
    then in private, he does something *else*!
A question I ask the learned men of our gathering:
    why those who order repentance, repent not, alas?
Obviously, they believe not in Judgment Day:
    such inversion—such fraud—in the works of the final Judge!
O God, the newly rich: put them on the back of their asses!
    They claim slaves, riches, and fast Arabian steeds![139]
You beggar at the door of the mosque, run to the tavern:
    the Master is dispensing a potion to enrich your heart!
His abundant kindness, though fatal to lovers,
    some arrive at that passion by His mystical light!
You angels, pray at the door of love's tavern with your beads:
    the nature of man fermented in that vat.[140]
      At dawn I heard a clamor from heavens: Wisdom said,
      "Perchance the angels are memorizing the poems of Hafez!"

Eighty-Four

I wish, they would unseal the tavern doors;
   I wish, they would untie the knot of contentions.
If the doors are sealed to please the virtuous,
   take heart—they'll open the doors in the name of God.
To delight the heart of the morning-drinking rendaan,
   many locked doors open—with the key-force of prayers.
Write the notice—the daughter of vine is dead:
   So! You Saghis,[141] split your hair in mourning![142]
The voice of harp was silenced,[143] by the demise of ruby wine:
   let the rivals weep—blood raining from their eyes.
The tavern doors are sealed, O God, pity;
   the doors to the house of deceits will open, a pity.
      Hafez, your garment, if you observe it tomorrow,
      the zonar[144] you wear under it will prove your bane![145]

Eighty-Five

For years our book[146] was in the pawn of wine:
    prosperity of the tavern, our teaching and prayer.
See the grace of my Master—we, the tippled—
    whatever we did, appeared fair in His eyes.
Whatever I know, you wash it off with wine:
    I heard the heavens—searching for a learned man!
Ask for "that"[147] from the beloved, if discerning at heart:
    I recommend it: I, an expert with roving eye![148]
Like a pair of compasses, my heart roves in all directions:
    yet in the circling it remains an erect rover.[149]
Sweet pain of love: the musician sings[150] such sad airs,
    the learned weep blood-tears from their eyes.
I blossomed from the ecstasy, like a flower by the brook:
    the shadow? That of the beloved shading me like a juniper.
My rosy Master,[151] talking of those wearing green attire[152]
    would not permit malice—lest, what stories he would tell?
        He would not buy into Hafez's counterfeit heart,
        the One who sees all hidden sins in clear light!

Eighty-Six

My heart, you're afflicted—your affliction will work miracles:
>   mid-night humility will fend off a thousand regrets.
Gladly take the flirtatious frown of the beloved like a lover:
>   one smiling wink, payment for a thousand sleights.
The curtain lifts to uncover the invisible[153]
>   for those who serve the mirror of life.
Love's healer is Jesus-breath and tender, yet
>   what cure can he offer if your pain is veiled?
Cast your lot with God—celebrate the event:
>   if your rival lack mercy, God has it in abundance.
Wearied of my sleeping luck: when awake—
>   will recite a morning prayer.
>>   Hafez fumes: beloved ignoring his plight;
>>   perhaps Zephyr to him will do duty!

Eighty-Seven

From her alley, blows the perfumed breeze of Norooz:[154]
    time to light up your heart to Zephyr to receive your wish.
Like a flower, if you've a little, spend it on pleasure:
    Midas suffered much for his lust of gold.
From the flower's cup the nightingale is so drunk with the ruby wine
    that he echoed the azured dome with the music of his victory song!
Go to the desert; wash away the dust of your woes;
    in the garden, learn from the nightingale the art of the ghazal!
Paradise is impossible under this azured dome:
    grasp the moment of pleasure in victory and health.[155]
To indulge the lover, abandon self indulgence:
    the grace is to abandon the position you hold!
Be a flower, burst forth from a blossom.[156]
    No more than a few days is the reign of Norooz.
I know not why the dove moans by the brook:
    does he suffer, day and night, like me in woes?
I hold a cup, pure as life; the Sufi finds flaws in wine!
    O God, may no wise man fall into the abyss of ill luck!
O Candle, sit desolate: your sweet love is parted now;
    it's decreed by fate: make peace with it or burn!
With the conceit of mind one cannot be robbed of pleasure!
    Come Saghi, the ignorant will enjoy it more—one day![157]
Drink your glorious wine in the company of Aasef,[158]
    a draught from your cup renews the world on time.
Hafez alone does not praise Khajeh Turanshah;
    for the praise of his patrons,[159] he demands gifts for Norooz.
      His presence, the pulpit of those pure of heart;
      His demeanor, the reward of the pious in victory.![160]

Eighty-Eight

The ignorant are in awe of our wondering eyes:
    I am what I appear to be—they must make up their minds!
The sage are the fixéd point of a pair of compasses,
    yet Love knows: they are lost—in their circles!
The exhibition[161] of her face is not only for my eyes!
    The sun and moon spin this very mirror round.
God made our covenant with those honey-lipped beauties:
    we are the creatures, and they, the creating gods.
Beggars we are, intent on wine and musicians:
    Ah! What if they will not pawn our ragged garment?
The sun cannot unite with the blind owl of night:
    in that mirror—the perplexed are perceptive men.
Bragging of love—or, complaining about the lover—what a fraud?
    Such lovers deserve a certain disaffection!
Unless your black eyes instruct me of the affairs of time:
    not all can be drunk and sober[162] at the same time!
Should the breeze carry your scent to the land of spirits,
    mind and soul, they'll scatter the kernel of life—a gift!
        If the pious cannot grasp the rendi of Hafez, what of it?
        Demons flee those reciting Koran!

Eighty-Nine

Early in the morning, after a night's drinking wine,
    I raise my wine cup to the music of castanet and harp.
For my reason, I laid my journey's provision with wine;
    from the city of its existence, I let reason run!
Mistress vintner gestured flirtatiously:
    I felt secure from the deceit of time.
Saghi whispered —with arched brows —
    "Oh, you, target of the arrow of reproach!
Will you profit from your beloved
    if you saw yourself in the middle of it?"
Go set this trap for another bird:
    Phoenix builds his nest—soaring high.
Narcissist self indulgence
    will not avail the love of God.
The musician, cup-bearer, and the companion, all himself:
    the thought of water and mud on the way—just a disguise.
Bring the ship of wine: cheerfully we will sail
    in this unbounded, shore-less sea.
        Our existence is an enigma, Hafez:
        questing its nature, only fable and charm.

Ninety

God forbid I deny wine when flowers blossom!
    I pretend to sapience; how can I commit such an act?
Where are you, O Musician? I'll spend all my learning and piety
    on harp, lyre, and the song of the flute!
The cacophony of the school house brings me a heavy heart.
    Oh, better spend time in the service of wine and my beloved.
When have you seen faith in fate—fetch the cup of wine
    so, I can spin the story of Kaavoos Key and Jam![163]
I fear not the black letters,[164] for in the Judgment Day
    by His grace I will survive a thousand such notes!
Where is the morning messenger: I'll complain of the night's separation
    to the one with lucky stars and good omens!
        This soul Friend entrusted to Hafez for keeps:
        one day I will see His face, returning that soul.

Ninety-One

We'll raise our hand of a night and pray;
    seek solace for your absence—elsewhere.
O help! My heart is sick because of the friends;
    fetch a healer to visit—give remedy!
The friend, who bled me and left annoyed for no reason—
    for Heaven's sake, bring him back for my pleasure!
Alas! The roots of pleasure all withered, show me the way to tavern?
    Possible—in that climate—it might take roots again.
My heart, ask rendaan for help—or else
    the task is hard! Beware and don't make mistakes.
Impatient angel's shadow is for naught!
    We ask for the shadow of the auspicious phoenix[165] for luck.
      Out of tune is my heart: where is sweet-tongued Hafez?
      We'll set to music and airs his songs and ghazals.

Ninety-Two

We chose our morning lesson at the door of the tavern:
    laid the fruits of our prayer at the door of the lover.
The harvest of a hundred pious men of wit
    set afire by this scar we've stamped on rabid heart.
The Eternal King gifted us the treasure of the sorrows of love
    ever since we arrived at this tattered mansion of woes.
Never! Not again will I consent to love another face of beauty.
    We sealed the doors of this house with His signet.
I will not wear the garment of guile—nor, continue in tiffs.
    Mine is a foundation built in the manner of rendaan.
The ship is unanchored, sailing on its own—alas!
    We risk our lives on the way of that peerless pearl!
Praise God! He was irreligious, without sentiments, just like us,
    the one who won the title of wisdom and learning from us!
        Assured of your grandeur, like Hafez,
        Alas, O God, we set a beggarly, alien ideal to lead.

Ninety-Three

We have not come to *this* place for pomp and ranks!
    We seek refuge from the evil of the event!
Travelers of the path of love, from the borders of not-being
    we traveled this long thoroughfare—to the state of being.[166]
We saw the tract of the fruit; from Eden
    we came, demanding this miracle weed.[167]
With such treasures, the ward of The Holy Spirit,
    as beggars, we've come to the door of our King.
Oh Ship of Grace, where is the charity of your anchor:
    born sinful—we come to this sea, filled with caritas.
O clouds, wash away with your rains our misdeeds,
    we have arrived for judgment with blackened sheets.[168]
        Hafez, toss away your woolen sack with equanimity;
        we have followed the caravan—with the fire of sighs.

Ninety-Four

Listen to my advice: hear and do not object;
  whatever the loving Adviser tells, accept it!
Enjoy your union with younger faces;
  the wily old age is on the prowl to snap.
For pleasure of both worlds, seek the company of lovers:
  one, a lesser commodity; the other, unbounded gift.
I'm in need of good company and the sound of lute
  to sing my pains with moaning notes, higher and low!
I'm of mind to stop drinking wine, commit no sins,
  if my plans become the plans of my fate!
Since our portion was doled out without our presence,
  if some of it is not to our satisfaction, what of it?
Pour wine and musk[169] in my cup of tulip, Saghi,
  the image of my lover's mole will not abandon my heart.
Fetch the cup, the lustrous pearl, Saghi;
  tell the jealous to observe the favor of Aasef[170] and die!
A hundred times have I set the goblet down and repented:
  alas, the amorous flirtations of the Saghi will not permit!
Twin-year aged wine, the beloved fourteen:
  that suffices me, the talk of the younger and older!
Who will steady and hold our disillusioned heart?
  Tell my story to the weary Majnoon in chains.[171]
    Hafez: no mention of repentance in this pleasure house:
    Lest the arrows of Saghi's arched-brows wound your heart![172]

Ninety-Five

If the gardener desires the company of flowers—for a day or two—
    for the bitter separation must bear the patience of a nightingale.
Oh heart, snared in the curls of the lover, do not despair:
    a clever bird caught in the trap must show patience!
A rebel rend and expedience, why should he care?
    laying plans and caution relate to those with possessions!
In the way of "tareeghat"[173] reliance on piety[174] and gnosis is heretical;
    the journeyer,[175] even with a thousand[176] talents, must yield to God.
With such tresses and face, no roving eyes to catch
    the face of jasmine, her jet black curls smelling of hyacinth.
Love her wined eyes and her coyness:
    this frenzied heart is mad for her black hair and tresses.
O Saghi—how long will you neglect circulating the vessel:
    the impossible cycle, when with lovers, must turn infinite.[177]
        Hafez drinks not his wine without a lute.
        A needy lover, why thinks he of such frills?

Ninety-Six

The thoughts of the nightingale with the flower, the lover:
    the flower mixing flirtation in the affair!
Flirtation isn't just to kill the lover!
    A noble master must show mercy to his vassal.
Time for the blood to wreak havoc in the heart of ruby—
    lest worthless shard replace the market of ruby!
The favor of the flower, the nightingale learned to sing; or else
    no song or music would break through his beak!
You, passing through the alley of our beloved,
    beware! The wall may topple over your head!
The absent one, a thousand hearts in his prayer:
    God, your protection, wherever he may be!
Talk of your welfare, sweet as it is, my heart,
    the path of the lover is precious, do not neglect!
Sufi is happy with the hand that tipped his hat;
    another cup or two, he'll have no steady hands!
        The heart of Hafez, addicted to your presence,
        delicately he bred this union—do not hurt him!

Ninety-Seven

O God, this laughing fresh flower you've entrusted me,
    I entrust you to keep my lover from evil eye.
Though distanced from the alley of faith a thousand ranks,
    may all the plagues of this world be spared her.
O West Wind, if you happen to breathe upon my beloved,
    I implore you: carry the love I bear to my beloved.
Delicately, with loving hands release the musk from her hair;
    it's the seat of many loving hearts: do not tousle it!
I shout: Tell my heart he has his claim on your face:
    treat gently those locks of hair and tresses.
Where her lips are toasted with wine,
    wretched the drunk—who is even aware of himself!
Cannot protect money or name once at the doors of the tavern,
    anyone drinking this draught will have to be laved at sea.[178]
Anyone afraid of woes: the pains of his love remain illicit.
    For us! Our head and her steps—or, our lips on her lips.
      The poems of Hafez, all mansions of insight:
      praise his soothing voice and delicate words.

Ninety-Eight

Yesternight, secretly told me a sagacious wit,
    "The tavern keeper's secrets cannot be kept any more.
Take the affairs of life easy, for it's in the nature of
    the world to make it hard for trying."
Then, he offered a cup, full of grace, full of light, its brilliance
    bringing Venus to a dance; with the lute she sang, "Your health."
Though bleeding heart, bring smile to your face—like the cup:
    not with a slight wound you might cry—like the harp!
Unless intimate, you will not hear the secret from this music;
    ears of the infidels[179] cannot bear the message of angels.
Listen to my advice and grieve not because of this world;
    I've given you a gem of an advice, if you hear me right.
In the court of love, no need for disputes:
    there, all organs must be eyes and ears.
In the realm of the wise, self-serving is no attribute.
    Speak with reasoned words, O you wise man, or remain silent!
    Saghi fetch the wine: Hafez's rendi understood
    Aasef,[180] the forgiver of crimes, concealer of faults.

Ninety-Nine

My heart breaks, ignorant am I, only a Dervish:
    whatever happened to that wandering game?
Like a willow, I shake, doubting my faith,
    my heart in the hands of an infidel beloved.
Impossible dreams of colossal[181] patience haunt my mind, alas,
    what is in the nature of this impossible thought?
I love it! Those flirtatious lashes, killer of piety,
    undulating sweet drinking water with sting!
A thousand drops of blood drip from the sleeve of a surgeon
    unless with skill he lays a hand on the wounded heart to stop it.
To the tavern door I saunter, weeping and dejected:
    I'm ashamed of the fruits of my self.
No life of Khezr,[182] nor the kingdom of Alexander remains:
    why quarrel, dervish, about this fickle world?
        Not any hand of any beggar will reach that high,[183] Hafez;
        find a treasure that surpasses that of Midas.

Hundred

Love affairs, youth, ruby-red wine,
    intimate gathering, good companion, constant imbibing,
sweet throated Saghi, divine voice of the musician,
    generous friends, loyal mate,
a beautiful woman, in purity, envy of the water of life,
    a lover, in perfection the envy of the full moon,
a pleasant pleasure dome, like Paradise,
    a rose-garden, like the Garden of Eden,
well intentioned petitioners, polite stewards,
    friends, secret keepers, responsive lovers,
rose colored, bitter, sharp, tasty, light wine,[184]
    chasers,[185] the ruby of the beloved,[186] the wine, raw ruby,
the flirtations of Saghi, wisely with a drawn sword,
    the beloved has spread her hair for my hunt.
Insightful, witty, like the sweet-spoken Hafez,
    kind exemplar of universal light, like Haji Ghavaam.[187]
        Any who denies this pleasure, happiness be lost for him:
        Any who rejects this assemblage, life be denied to him.

Hundred and One

I openly declare, happy of my divulgence:
    I'm a slave to love, free of both worlds.
I'm a bird in Paradise, what can I say of separations:
    how did I fall into the trap of this misfortune?
I was an angel, the Garden of Eden my home;
    Adam brought me to this broken land: made it my home.
Shadow of the Tree of Life,[188] consolation of angels, and the brook:[189]
    I have forgotten all—because of you!
On the slate of my heart, no letter, but alpha, figure of the friend.[190]
    What can I do: the Master taught me—only that one?
The sign of my luck, no astrologer could read:
    O God, from Mother Earth, what ill star I inherit?
Since becoming slave to the door of love's tavern,
    every breath brings sorrow anew to my pleasure.[191]
        Wash away the tears of Hafez with the brush of your hair:
        Lest this constant flood wash his roots away!

Hundred and Two

For years I followed the religion of rendaan,
    till I went to prison, decree of the wisdom of my avarice.
Unwitting—I reached the nest of Phoenix,
    traversing that path with the help of Hoopoe.[192]
Cast your shadow upon my heart, O you flowing treasure:
    I've destroyed this house in hopes of our pleasure!
I repented: promised never to kiss the lips of Saghi;
    Now! Now I bite my lips for listening to such an ignoramus.
Break your old habits: seek fulfillment, for
    I've won my addictions from your tousled hair.
The matter of intoxication or sobriety—no choice of ours;
    whatever the eternal king's order, I obeyed.
From the Eternal grace I look for Paradise:
    yet, I've been known to be a door keeper to taverns!
When old, my head filled with the story of Joseph;
    reward of my patience: I suffered in the house of woes.
Early rising, conscious of health, like Hafez,
    whatever I did, it was from the grace of Koran.
        In the court of ghazal I sit in the place of honor—no wonder
        for years I've paid homage to the court of kings![193]

Hundred and Three

Though old, frail, and tired of life,
    remembering your face turns me into a youth again.
Thanks be God! Whatever I've asked Him,
    I've succeeded beyond my expectations.
Oh, you young rose-bush of luck and means:
    you have made me into the nightingale of this world.
At first, I was oblivious[194] to my soul and my being:
    it was in your school of woes—I became so wise.
My stars point me to the tavern,
    the more I practice *this*, the more I receive of *that*![195]
That day the doors to apprehension opened wide into my heart,
    when I became a supplicant in the court of my Master.
On the pathway to eternal blessing, to the throne of fate,
    I went to indulge the hearts of my friends with a goblet of wine.
Ever since the temptation of your eyes have ensnared me,
    I've become immune to the mischief promised in Parousia.[196]
I am not agéd by years, but my beloved's[197] want of faith;
    my life passes on, but the beloved ages me!
        Yesternight, Grace whispered glad tidings: "Hafez return";
        "I have guaranteed you the forgiveness of your sins."

Hundred and Four

I'm a lover of beautiful faces and flowing hair;
  slave to amorous eyes and pure, unsullied wine.
You said, "Tell us about the secrets of the Promise Day."[198]
  I said, "I'll tell, when I have had—a draught of wine!"
I'm a Man of Paradise, but in this journey, now
  I'm a slave of the love of those young beauties.
No escaping the burning and light[199] when in love:
  like a candle, I'm well versed; do not try to scare me!
Shiraz, a paradise of ruby lips and a mine of beauty,
  but I'm an impoverished smith, and that's my lot!
Myriad besotted eyes caress my sight in the city:
  I'm tippled with no need to drink any wine.
Lavished full with flirtatious nymphs from six directions;
  poverty prevents me, though I'm a customer of all six directions!
If fortune allow, and I travel to my beloved,
  the tresses of the nymph will clear dust from my rug!
    Hafez, my delicate sense desires a presence;
    I possess not a mirror, the source of my sighs!

Hundred and Five

The path to the tavern, well swept and sprinkled with water,
    the Master sitting high, issuing invitation to young and old.
wine-bearers, his servants, all at his service,
    but from his head, the canvas touching the heavenly skies:[200]
the dazzle of the cup dimming the light of moon,
    the face of the serving Saghis—sun-burnt through,
the bride of fate with thousand flirtations in the bridal chamber,
    tousling her hair,[201] spraying rose-water on the leaves of roses,
the angel of mercy, opting for the pleasure of a cup,
    spraying the faces of nymphs and angels with the draught,
from the excitement and revelry of the sweet lovers
    pouring sweetness, jasmine scattered, viol playing;[202]
I greeted the Master, and he said with a smiling face,
    "O you intoxicated, beggar: wine crazed;
what a madness you did—for lack of good sense and will?
    Treasure house you forsook—took up a tent in a dump;
I fear the state of wakefulness will be denied you;
    you've slept in the arms of the sleepy fate.
Come to the tavern, Hafez, so I can offer you,
    thousand rows of already accepted prayers!
The Dome,[203] a spare horse of Shah Nosrat Al-din,[204]
    come, see, the Majesty is intent on riding!
        Wisdom, a mysterious inspirer in acquiring honors,
        sends a thousand kisses to you from the roof of Dome."[205]

Hundred and Six

Love's musician! What wondrous sound and melody:
    composition of each note he plays, soothing!
May never the sound of lover's moan disappear:
    its music pleasing, its air healing!
Our Master, though without gold or power,
    has a forgiving nature and a giving heart.
Honor my heart, this insignificant sugar-loving fly
    since becoming your devotee, an eagle's splendor its right.
Not far from justice when a king inquires
    after a neighbor, a beggar, by his side.
I cried blood from my eyes and asked physicians, they said,
    "It's the disease of love—painful remedies must be employed!"
Do not learn cruelty from your flirtations, for in the religion of love
    every action has its reward, every ill deed its punishment.
Wonderfully said that beautiful Christian, wine-worshipper tot,
    "Drink to the health of the one who is pleasant!"
        O King, Hafez of your court is coming to his final end!
        From your mouth, he is begging a prayer!

Hundred and Seven

I swear to Khajeh,[206] and our old friendship pact:
    my early morning prayers are for your weal.
My tears, greater than Noah's flood,
    could not wash away the stamp of your love from my heart.
Come! Make a bargain: buy this broken heart;
    though broken, it's worth a hundred thousand—right!
The words of the ant to Aasef[207] were long, and befitting
    that Khajeh lost Jam's[208] signet and did not seek it.
O heart, never lust after the infinite favor of the friend.
    Since you lay claims to love, lose your head—readily!
Endeavor in truth, let the sun shine from your breath:
    Since, from falsity, the first morning[209] fell into exact shame!
I'm a wild wanderer of the hills and dale because of you,
    yet, where is your mercy, and why not loosen your sash?
        Don't be vexed, Hafez: seek not shelter from a sweetheart!
        How can you blame the garden if this weed does not grow?

Hundred and Eight

Whoever cares for the people of God,
    God will care for him—come hail or flood.
I'll not tell the story of the friend except to the self of the friend,
    for a friend keeps the words of a friend!
My love! Live such, if your feet slide,
    your angel may hold you up with the two hands of your prayer!
In the hopes of the Lover keeping covenant,
    hold on the thread: He'll hold on the thread!
O West Wind, if you happen to see my heart in the beloved's tresses,
    kindly advise it to keep hold of its place.
When I begged "Keep my heart," the answer came,
    "What can I do? May God—keep it!"
I'll sacrifice my life, gold, and my heart to a friend
    who keeps the right of talk—about our faith and love.
        Where is the dust of your feet on this path, so Hafez
        may keep it as a memento of the breeze?

Hundred and Nine

Let's pass by the path to enter the tavern:
  for a draught we are all in need of that door.
The first day we professed to rendi and love,
  the condition is to stay within the path—no straying.
When the throne and scepter of Jam[210] is in ruins,
  do not drink from the bitter cup of regrets, drink wine.
The thought of my hands on the beloved sash
  makes my heart fill up with ruby red blood.
Preacher, stop offering advice to those crazed with love:
  with lover's alley dust upon us, we'll not consider Paradise.
Since Sufis are in dance and mimics,
  we, too, partake of their gimmicks!
From a drop of wine from your cup, the dirt grew pearls and rubies;
  pity us, the poor! We are less than dirt in your eyes.
    Hafez, the path does not lead to the turrets of the palace:
    We'll do with the dust of this doorway, any day!

Hundred and Ten

We expected friendship from a friend:
    whatever we thought, it was a mistake!
For the tree of friendship to bear fruit,
    we went and planted a seed.
Bickering is not in the tradition of Dervishes:
    otherwise, we would have untold contentions.
The gaze in your eyes held the deceit of warring,
    we made the error and took it for peace.
The flower of your beauty was not self-achieved:
    we, too, had a hand in wishing you such.
Events did happen, no one complained,
    we never abandoned the side of respect!
        Hafez, you gave your heart freely:
        we did not send the sentry for that!

Hundred and Eleven

I have the decree of the Master, an old adage:
>   it's profane to drink wine without a companion.
I'll rend my garment of duplicity: what can I do?
>   Conversation of the malicious is painful torture to my soul.
Unless the lips of the beloved feed me a draught,
>   I've been a resident at the door of the tavern for many years.
Lest my long service the beloved remember not:
>   O morning breeze, remind my lover of our old pledges.
In a hundred years, if you happen upon my dust;
>   my decayed bones will rise, dancing from the clay.
The beloved first stole our heart with a thousand hopes:
>   obviously, the generous never forget a promise!
Tell the blossom: grieve not—if still in hiding;
>   morning breath and the breeze of the wind are your help.
For a cure, my heart, knock at another door;
>   a lover's pain: incurable by a physician's remedy.
Learn to hold the essence of wisdom to take with you:
>   the tax collector will take your gold and silver.
Painful is a trap unless God's grace comes to help:
>   otherwise, no one can win with the cursed Satan.
>   Hafez, if you lack gold and silver, be grateful;
>   what surpasses meek nature and beautiful words?

Hundred and Twelve

Determined to repent, this morning I said, "Self, consult a magician!"[211]
    What can I do? The spring is here, time to break contrition.
I'll tell you straight: I cannot see
    how others drink wine, and I remain an observer!
Like a blossom with a smile, remembering the gala of the king,
    I'll take the cup and rend my garment in pure rapture!
At the time of passing the tulip around, have my head examined
    if I remove myself from the center of merriment!
From the face of a friend, like a flower, my wishes blossom;
    I assign the head of my enemy to hit a boulder.
I'm the beggar of my tavern: observe me when I'm drunk:
    I flirt with the universe and reign over the stars.
Not me! I lack a tradition of parsimony:
    why would I blame the wining rendaan?
Like a Sultan, I'll settle a nymph on a throne of flowers,
    weave ringlets of jasmine and hyacinth for her lace and garter.[212]
        Hafez is weary of drinking wine sequestered.
        I'll divulge his secret thoughts to the tune of lyre and pipes.

Hundred and Thirteen

The unfaithful one, I'm the dirt of his path;
    I kiss the ground and beg forgiveness from his feet.
God forbid I bemoan his cruelty:
    I'm a well wishing servant, loyal slave!
I've tied my long hopes to the curls of your hair:
    God forbid in urgent of need I cut my hopes away!
I'm a speck of dust, your alley my happy residence;
    my fear, dear friend: the wind will blow me away unawares.
At dawn, the Master handed me a discerning cup:[213]
    in the mirror of wine, I was made aware of your beauty.[214]
I am a Sufi[215] in the house of the wisdom of Holiness,
    but for present, the tavern is my home.
Stand up! Come to the tavern with me, a beggar;
    see my high position in that circle!
You passed by, drunk, with no thought of Hafez!
    Oh, that my sighs catch up with your life!
        I loved it when at dawn the King of the East[216] was saying,
        "With all my majesty, I'm the slave of Tooran Shah!"[217]

Hundred and Fourteen

Free of sorrow and wined, our hearts lost,
  we're an intimate of Love's and a companion of cup.
When at us arrows of blame are hurled—
  solace in the brow of the beloved we take.
O tulip, you've borne the pain of a morning's draught;
  we are the flower,[218] born with that pain.
The Master, if displeased with our contrition,
  tell him: refine the wine, we are full of regrets.
Only you're in charge, O help, my Master.
  We admit: we are lost wayfarers.
The tulip sees only the wine—the cup in center:
  notice this pain, filling our broken hearts.
    You asked: what of all your rainbow of colors and wit?
    You're mistaken: we are simple and clear slates.

Hundred and Fifteen

The glorious Phoenix[219] will fall into our trap
   if you happen to saunter our way.
Like a bubble, I'll throw my hat in the air
   if the picture of your face appear in my cup.
The night our wish-moon rises in the horizon,
   a dazzle of light will flood our lives.[220]
In your court the wind is given no audience:
   how is it possible to send our greetings, then?
My soul the ransom of her lips, I thought
   a drop of her well-water would reach us.
The thought of your hair advised us, "beware";
   abundant such preys to fall in our trap.
Do not leave dispirited through these doors: cast a lot.[221]
   Perchance, the lot will bear our name on it!
      Any breath taken in your alley, Hafez,
      blows the scent of roses to our face.

Hundred and Sixteen

The only friend, free of malice, nowadays,
  is a cup of cleared wine and a collection of ghazals.
Go lightly: the pathway to virtue is far and narrow;
  take the cup: the precious life is quite matchless.
I'm not the only soul bored by inaction:
  the tedium of the cleric is also caused by the art of inaction!
In the eyes of the discerning, on this turbulent road,
  the world and the affairs of life are unstable—.
Hold on to the locks of a sweetheart and quit telling stories,
  for good-or-bad luck is the influence of the heavenly stars.[222]
My heart's desire was the consummation of our love.
  Alas! Death in the path of life is the robber of all desires.
   Never will they find him sober:
   our Hafez is drunk from eternal wine.

Hundred and Seventeen

Listen to my words to escape the bitterness of woes:
    insisting on a day—not ordained—will fill your heart with woes.
At the end, you'll be the clay of the potter's wheel:
    now think of a clay pot to fill—up to brim.
If you're one of those yearning for Paradise,
    now seek pleasure with a few angel-born human beings!
You cannot affect greatness on a whim
    unless all the parts of greatness are gathered in.
Much honor to you, O Khosro, Sheereen's lover,
    were you to look kindly on the broken Farhaad.[223]
Your heart will receive the blessing—we will see—
    only if from many complex images you make a simple form.[224]
Your affairs to Grace cede, Hafez,
    to enjoy God's grace, bestowed on you.
        O Morning Breeze, serve Khajeh Jajal Al-Din[225]
        and release jasmine and lily on the face of this earth.

Hundred and Eighteen

O You, the apple of my eye, listen to the words I must say:
    as your cup is full of wine, drink and share.
On the path of love, abundant temptation of Satan:
    come forth and heed the message of the Divine Angel.[226]
Spoiled is the song, the music of happiness all but gone:
    O harp howl, O tambourine shout.
Rosaries nor sackcloth yield the pleasure of being drunk:
    request this pleasure only from the wine seller.
"Old Masters of words speak from experience," I said.
    "Young lad, may you be an old man, listen to my advice."
Love does not put much stock on wisdom:
    deny it if you desire to caress the tresses of the beloved.
With friends, what need to deny life or money;
    give your life a hundred fold to a friend who listens to advice.
Saghi! May your cup never remain empty, without clear wine,[227]
    but look kindly upon me, a lees drinker sot!
        Drunk with wealth, passing clad in golden robes,
        swear to God to give the sack-clothed[228] Hafez a kiss!

Hundred and Nineteen

Tall and flirtatious, my designing beloved
    in one breath cut short the story of my virtue.
Did you notice, my love Agéd, with virtue and learning,
    what my lusting eyes have wrought upon my self?
I fear, with such a weakened conviction I bear,
    the altar of your eyes will take away my prayers.
I said, "I'll wear the garment of deceit as a sign of my love."
    My tears betrayed me, revealing my secrets!
The friend is wined and does not mention the rivals:
    well remembered,[229] my beggar-loving Saghi!
O God, when will the Zephyr blow, the breeze
    bringing the scent of grace as my aid.
Now, my tears paint a picture on the water!
    When will my facts match my metaphors?
Inside, laughing I cry like a candle
    to see what my burning and yielding do to your stony heart!
You ascetic! Since your prayers are left unanswered,
    join me in nightly wining—in my secrets and in my needs.
      Hafez is drowning in tears: Zephyr you tell
      the forgiving king—at once, unforgiving of his enemies.

Hundred and Twenty

The lover mocks: you left to see the spectacle of the new moon;
    the shame of the moon next to my brows,[230] and out you go!
For long, your heart a slave of our tresses:[231]
    will you neglect, now, your own beloved?
Do not barter away our tresses with the perfume of your mind,
    where a thousand measure of musk is worth a whit![232]
The seeds of faith and love in this ancient farm
    become manifest only at the time of harvest.
Saghi, fetch the wine, and I'll tell you the mystery
    of the ancient path of stars and the secrets of the new moon.
The crest shape of every new moon shows
        The crown of Seeyaamak and the loss of Zoo's hat![233]
            Hafez, His Highness the Master is a refuge of affection.
            Read the lesson of love to him—and hear him answer!

Hundred and Twenty-One

The rose garden bursts in delight of colors: where is my beloved?
    The west wind sends delicate gusts: where is my wine?
Each flower a child of a beauty remembered, but
    where is the discerning ear, where the sapient eye?
This pleasure-fest is lacking in ambergrist and musk.
    O sweet-scented breeze, where is the musk of the beloved's tresses?
O morning breeze, I cannot bear the vainglory of the flower.
    This, the end of my patience, for God's sake, where is the lover?
The candle, if of a morning boasts to look like you,
    just the enemy is wagging its tongue; where is the sharp dagger?
The lover asked if I did not desire a kiss from her ruby lips!
    I'm dying of this desire, but where is the power and my will?
      Although Hafez is a treasure-house of words, yet for
      the woes of this ill natured world, where is our wordsmith?

Hundred and Twenty-Two

Devoted to you I am, and I know you know it.
    You see without looking and read the unwritten word.
How can a blamer discern the love between lovers?
    Unseeing eyes cannot perceive hidden, private secrets.
Tousle the hair and bring Sufi to a dance;
    scatter a thousand idols from each patch of his rags.
The key to our affairs is in the brow of the lover.
    For God's sake! Tarry for a moment: open the knot on your brows.
The angel, prostrate at the feet of Adam, intended it for you in the future;
    in your goodness, the angel saw a grace beyond human faces.[234]
The light in our eyes blazing by the breeze from the beloved's tresses.
    O God protect this lot from the ill winds of despair.
Such pity the revelry of dawn is lost in the morning sleep;
    my heart, you never value time unless you are in need.
Weary of your companions? It is not expedient;
    carry present troubles in the memory of times of comfort.
        The thought of her curls is beguiling, Hafez.
        Beware of trying to turn an impossible curve.

Hundred and Twenty-Three

Two shrewd lovers, heavy with agéd wine,
    free, a book at hand, and the corner of a garden:
I will not barter this state for this world or the other,
    even if the men get into my nerves constantly.
Exchanging the corner of contentment for the treasures of this world
    is selling the Egyptian Joseph[235] to his lowest bidder.
Let's try it, to keep this place[236] successful
    by the virtue of someone like you, or the debauchery of me!
In gale of the events one cannot distinguish
    in this garden if there ever was a rose or a jasmine bush!
In the cup's mirror discern the mysteries of the plan:
    none remembers such strange events at any time!
This hot wind—sweeping our garden:
    it's a wonder there is still a scent of rose and the color of eglantine.
Patience, my dear heart: the Just One will never abandon
    such a dear gem to the hands of Ahriman.[237]
        The health of our world is wasted in this venture, Hafez:
        where are the thoughts of a philosopher—the Brahma's will?[238]

Hundred and Twenty-Four

From juniper at dawn the nightingale sang[239]
    in Pahlavi[240] lessons on spiritual discernment:
saying, "Come, see the rose manifest the fire of Moses[241]
    and learn from the bush the point of God's unity.
The birds in the garden are witty and know rhyming well,
    till Khajeh[242] sips wine, listening to ghazals in Pahlavi.[243]
Except for the story of the cup, Jamsheed[244] took nothing from this world;
    take heed and never set your heart on matters of this life.
Listen to this strange story from the altered luck:
    the beloved killed us with the breath of Jesus![245]
What a wonderful life is a ragged mat, beggary, and peaceful sleep;
    this luxury not befitting the throne of kings!
Your flirtatious eyes the cause of ruination of many homes.
    May you never be only half-drunk: you go wonderfully full drunk!
The old Master, how graciously he told the boy,
    "The light of my eye: you only reap what you sow!"
        Saghi! Was the pension of Hafez increased
        to rattle the fake locks under the bandana of Molavi?[246]

Hundred and Twenty-Five

You, the untutored, be discerning through knowledge:
    unless a follower, how can you be a leader?
In the school of truth, tutored by the author of love,
    my son, try hard: you will be a father one day![247]
Like a wayfarer, wash off the copper from your elemental self
    to discover the alchemy of love, becoming gold!
Sleep and food, you can do with less:
    You will apprehend Self when freed from eating and sleep.
If the light of the love of Truth graces your heart and soul,
    by God, you will shine brighter than the sun of the heavens.
For a moment dive into the sea of your God, but never doubt:
    water of the seven seas cannot wet one strand of your hair.
From your feet to your head, all becoming the light of God,
    if on the way to God, you become feet-less and without a head.
If your gaze is at the justification of the Almighty God,
    no doubt remains—so you will become insightful.
When your being is turned up-side-down,
    never worry when you're turned around!
      Hafez, if aiming at the consummation of love,
      you must become a servant of the learned men.[248]

Hundred and Twenty-Six

My heart, if you abandon that well on the beloved's chin,[249]
  where you go, soon you'll feel the remorse.
Beware! In surrendering to the temptation of your reason,
  like Adam, you'll have to forsake Eden.
Perhaps, you will be refused water from the well spring of the Firmament
  if you return still thirsty from the spring of this earth.[250]
I long to have a glimpse of your face in the morning light;
  like the shining sun, you arrive at my door.
Like the morning breeze, I'll tend to you with all my might
  to open your blossom into a happy, smiling rose.
In the night-gloom of your absence, my patience wears:
  it's time to come to my door like the shining moon.
Two hundred brooks run in your passageway from my eyes.
  It's possible! You may come out in a happier mood!
    Hafez, think not that handsome Joseph[251]
    will return to release you from your woes!

Hundred and Twenty-Seven

Come through the convent doors: illumine our night into a day;
    scent with perfume the assembly of the holy men.
If the preacher advises you to forsake loving,
    give him a cup of wine: tell him to refresh his mind.[252]
Trust my body and soul to the eyes and brow of my beloved:
    come, you come! View the arch and that spectacle.
The stars of a night of separation cast no light:
    come to the roof of the castle—light the moon.
Tell the treasurer of Paradise to take the earth from this assembly:
    a gift to the Garden, to burn it as incense in the censer.
I am weary of wearing mozavvajeh[253] and this garment:
    with a wink of your eye transform me from a Sufi to a ghalandar.[254]
Since lovers of the meadow, you're permitted by beauty
    to flirt with jasmine, and parade in front of juniper.
Meddling *self* tells many tales, Saghi:
    you keep your composure and pour your wine.
The curtain of insight became the light of life;
    come and light the home-tent of the sun.
The lust for the sugar of our consummation will not do;
    rush, direct me to your sugar-like ruby lips.
Kiss the lip on the goblet, then pass it to the winers,
    at this point, wet the wit of your companions with wine.
        After participation in pleasure, and the love of beauties,
        among your tasks, memorize the verses of Hafez.

Hundred and Twenty-Eight

My friends: better tend to pleasure while the rose blooms,
    it's the word of the lover, and we'll drink with pleasure.
No generosity in any one, and the time for gaiety passing;
    the remedy is selling our prayer rug for wine!
The air is perfumed, perfect, O Lord:
    send us a beauty to drink rosy wine, honoring her face!
Creator of the organ of heavens, the enemy of the learned man:[255]
    why should we not bemoan this woe and remain still?
Rose fermented—and, we did not dilute it with wine;
    therefore, we boil with the fire of regret and lust.
We drink from the cup of tulip a metaphoric wine.
    God forbid![256] Without a musician and wine, we are all drunk.
      Hafez, who will hear this mysterious state of affairs?
      I'm a nightingale, falling silent during the time of roses.[257]

Hundred and Twenty-Nine

Oh, come let's scatter rose petals and fill the cup with wine;
    let's tear the ceiling of the universe and create a new one.
If the army of woes is intent on shedding the lovers' blood,
    Saghi and I will ride together and uproot the army's foundation!
We'll pour rose water in the bowl of purple wine;
    we'll in censer pour the sweetness of the scented wind.
Musician, play a sweet tune, if you are holding the harp:
    we'll sing ghazals, clapping hands, and dance in rapture.
Morning breeze, blow the ashes of my being to my beloved:
    perchance, we may have a glimpse of her face.
One lies about his wisdom, another weaves superstition:
    come, let's take these claims to the court of our Judge.
If you seek the Garden of Eden, then come to tavern:
    one day, we'll launch you in the Kosar Pool[258] from your wine urn!
      Eloquence and good singing are not valued in Shiraz:
      Come Hafez! Let's find us another town!

Hundred and Thirty

A lifetime since we set our path, lamenting you:
    we've set aside both the faces and duplicity of men.
The arches and balconies of the school house, all a pandemonium
    we left for the cup and the beautiful face of Saghi.
We've given our being to those two magical jonquils;[259]
    we've given our heart to those two Indian hyacinths.[260]
A life time has passed in hopes of a sign:
    we've kept our sight on the two corners of the brows.
We haven't placed our hope of well being[261] with armies,
    nor have we laid our arms on a throne of monarchy.
Come morning, we'll see what the beloved's eyes will do—;
    again, we've appealed to the wink of a talisman.
Without your insurgent hair, I, in the melancholy of pain,
    like a violet[262] have bent my head on my knees.
Hopeful, like a melancholy watcher of the moon,
    we have set our supplicant eyes upon the lover's arched brows.
        Hafez, you ask where your befuddle heart rests:
        in the curls of your beloved's tresses!

Hundred and Thirty-One

Mourning the Garden of Eden is the private affair of Darvishes.[263]
>   The yeast of grace is in the service of Darvishes.
The treasure of solitude that has magical talisman:
>   conquering it is in the focus of the grace of Darvishes.
The Castle in the Garden, seraphim[264] its keeper of gates,
>   is a glimpse of the pleasure garden of Darvishes.
Whatever turns to gold—from its luminance—that black heart
>   is the alchemical talk of Darvishes.
The crown-pride of the sun is humbled—
>   compared to the honor of the station of Darvishes.
Any state, free of the fear of dissolution:
>   hear it right! That's the state of Darvishes.
Kings are the object of worship in this world, but
>   its effect is the servant-hood of the honorable Darvishes.
The purpose kings pray to attain:
>   its genesis is in the mirror of the mien of Darvishes.
From border to border reigns the army of cruelty, but
>   from the beginning to the end is the time of Darvishes.
You, rich man: do not show all this haughtiness because
>   your head and your gold fly on the wings of Darvishes.
The treasures of Gharoon,[265] still sinking in anger,
>   be advised that, too, is due to the honor of Darvishes.
Hafez, if you seek the water of eternal life,
>   its source is the doorway dust of the home of Darvishes.
>   I'm the slave of Aasef,[266] who has
>   the face of a master, the soul of Darvishes.

Hundred and Thirty-Two

No one has yet seen your face, and the nightingale your protector;
    still in blossom, and a hundred nightingales at your service.
If I came to your alley, no wonder!
    Like me, thousands of lonely people dwell in that alley.
In love there is no difference between a monastery and the tavern:
    wherever, it's filled with the beloved's light.
Where the monastery stands
    is the belfry of the monks and the name of the cross.
Who fell in love that the beloved did not tend to him?
    O master, though there's no pain, yet there is a healer.
        After all, the voice of Hafez is not heard in vain.
        It is both a strange tale and a magical tradition.

Hundred and Thirty-Three

Pleasure, talk, a garden, and the spring time, that is all I need.
    Where is Saghi? Tell us, what reason for the delay?
Any moment of pleasure at hand, seize it;
    who knows the end of the affair!
The essence of life hangs from a single hair, beware:
    deal with your own sorrows, what of the universe's woes?
The meaning of the water of life and of paradise
    is no more than the banks of a brook and tasty wine!
The sober and the drunk are from the same tribe:
    who shall steal our heart; what has been written for our lot?
How can the silent firmament know the secret behind the curtain?
    Friend, what is your quarrel with the owner of that curtain?
If the sins of His creatures are unforgivable, then
    what of the forgiveness and mercy of the Creator?
        Preacher, Hafez and the Kosar wine,[267] both require a goblet;
        meanwhile, who knows what is the will of the Creator?

Hundred and Thirty-Four

O God, from whose nest comes this smiling candle?[268]
    We are burning: I ask whose beloved is she?
Now, ruination of my heart and my religion to know in
    whose embrace the beloved is—and whose bedfellow at night?
The wine of her ruby lips away from my lips:
    whose soul wine—promising whom to serve her mead?
For heaven's sake, inquire who has the license
    to speak to that lit candle of luck?
Everyone spins a yarn, yet it's unknown
    to which story her fragile heart sways.
O God, that shaah-vash-eh, maah-rokh-eh, zohreh jabeen,[269]
    whose precious pearl, whose single gem is she?
        I said, "Oh, the mad heart of Hafez without you."
        With a smile on her lip, she asked, "Mad for whom?"

Hundred and Thirty-Five

My sweet moon[270] left me this week, but it feels a year.
  What do you know of separation? It's a terrible condition!
The reflection of my pupil fell upon her beautiful face:
  I saw my reflection, mistaking it for her black mole.
I can still smell breath of milk on her sweet, sugary lips,
  in flirtation, each eye-lash, a killer!
You, a model of generosity in our town:
  alas, negligent in the affairs of strangers in town!
Never again will I doubt the fact of atomy:
  your mouth a resolute reason for that.
Glad tidings we had of your visit our way.
  Don't change your good intentions: it's a good presage.
    How long will he have to pull the mountain of separation?
    Poor Hafez! From sorrow his body is a writing reed![271]

Hundred and Thirty-Six

The path of love cannot be shun by anyone:
    on the way, but for dying, no likely remedy.
Any moment giving your heart to loving is rewarding:
    doing good-works requires no hesitation.[272]
Do not scare us with the taboo of reason, bring us wine.
    In our town the judge[273] musters no dominion!
Could you ask your eyes, who's killing us?
    My love, it's not the fault of fate, nor the crime of stars.
The beloved should be seen only with pious eyes—like a crescent moon:
    not any eye is allowed to see the rising of that beauty!
Take a chance in the path of rendi, for that sign,
    like the path of treasures, is not known to just anyone!
      The tears of Hafez never affected you:
      I love a heart that's not less than granite.

Hundred and Thirty-Seven

At dawn, the nightingale told the new born flower:
    "Do not demure. In this garden, many like you have blossomed."
The rose laughed, "We'll not be offended by truth, but
    no lover is known to use harsh words with his beloved!"
If hoping for a draught of wine from that golden[274] cup,
    how many pearls must you pierce with the force of your lashes?[275]
The scent of love will never reach the one
    unwilling to wash his face with the dust of the door of the tavern.
In the Garden of Eram,[276] one morning—for the balmy air
    the tresses of hyacinth complained to Zephyr.
I asked, "O king of the throne: where is your discerning[277] cup?"
    He replied, "Alas, that wide-awake world is asleep again!"
Praise of love is not uttered in words.
    Saghi, fetch wine, and quit this idle talk.
        Tears of Hafez cast patience and wisdom to the sea.
        What could he do? The bitter sorrow of love would not hide.

O nightingale, cry if intent on loving:
    we're a pair, madly in love, our fate, crying.
Where breeze blows from the lover's tresses,
    what need scenting the air with Tartarian musk?
Bring wine to stain the garment of guile:
    we're drunk with pride, famed for sobriety!
Lusting after your locks, not a task for anyone:[278]
    lying with the hair is the path of ayyaari![279]
A hidden, delicate magic, the source of love:
    its name is not ruby lips—or green growing![280]
Beauty of the body is not in eyes, nor hair or mole on cheek:
    a thousand delicate points relate to the art of loving.
True ghalandaraan[281] will not buy for a farthing
    the satin garment of the man devoid of learning.
True! It's formidable to arrive at your threshold, but
    ascending to the heights of mastery is exacting!
At dawn, I dreamt of the flirtations of your eyes.
    Behold! The moment of dreaming was superior to wakefulness.
        Don't torment your lover with complaints, Hafez; let go.
        Eternal salvation is in harmlessness.

Hundred and Thirty-Nine

Privacy is wondrous when the lover is mine
    so I may not flame and she become the light of the convention.
I cannot want that signet of Solomon[282]
    handled by Ahriman,[283] from time to time.
O Lord, may not in the privacy of fulfillment
    the rival succeed and privation be my lot.
Tell the majestic Phoenix[284] to lift her shadow of honors
    from where the nightingale is valued less than a vulture.
What need of eager rhetoric? The torrid fire of heart
    is apparent from the flaming words!
I cannot get your face out of my mind:
    the heart of a stranger yearns for his native land.
      Like a lily, if Hafez has ten tongues[285]
      like a bloom he'll seal his lips in your presence.

Hundred and Forty

Get a life, preacher! Why this cacophony?
    My heart has misled me; what has happened to you?
Among those God created from the void
    there's a delicate moment no creature can know.
Unless my lips reach communion with the beloved's like a flute,
    the advice of the whole world is only wind in my ears!
The beggar of your alley is independent of the eight paradises:
    a slave to your love is free from here and here-after.[286]
Though being Love's drunk has brought ruination, yet
    the foundation of my being is created upon that ruination.
My heart, do not bemoan the cruelty of the Lover:
    it's the Lover who has portioned you such a lot.
        Hafez, stop weaving tales and breathing spells;
        I remember much of your myths and talismans!

Hundred and Forty-One

My heart, you grace us not with your presence;
    you've all the tools, but deny their use.
You've the bat at hand, but refuse to hit the polo ball;
    you have the hawk of victory on hand, but refuse to hunt.
Plenty of blood pulsing through your heart, but
    in practice refuse attention to your love.
The breath of your disposition unscented with musk because,
    unlike Zephyr, you refuse to pay a visit to your love.
I fear you shall have no share of flowers from this garden,
    refusing to suffer thorns from its bushes of roses.
Hidden dormant in your sleeves, abundant musk, but
    refusing to sacrifice it to scent a beauty's tresses.
Saghi, delicately you pour wine on the ground,
    never heeding the danger of morrow's wine-headache.
        Hafez, leave! All profess slavery to the ruling king,
        but you; you refuse to do it even once!

Hundred and Forty-Two

The voice in the tavern said this morning in good will,
    "Come again: you're an old resident of this court.
Like Jamsheed, drink from us to discern from the glow
    on the magical cup[287] the secrets of this world and the other!"
At the tavern doors stand the ghalandar[288] rendaan[289]
    who give and receive the imperial crown.
A vagabond, stone for pillow[290] and the seven planets his cover,
    then, notice the hand of might and the rank of puissance.
Our head and the door of the tavern, its roof
    reaching the heavens—but such low walls around!
Do not set a course in this matter unless the Master[291] is present:
    many unlit paths; fear the danger of mishaps.
My heart, if they bestow you a beggar's crown,
    your smallest realm will be from moon to the fish.[292]
You do not understand the state of beggary: do not lose
    your rank of Khajeh and the company of Tooran Shah.[293]
        Hafez, glean from this story the shame of vanity in greed:
        what have you done to deserve a place in Paradise?

Hundred and Forty-Three

I said: I yearn for you. She said: The yearning will pass!
    I said: Be my moon. She said: If it shines!
I said: learn the ways of devotion from those who love;
    she said: rare are such deeds by those who're lovely.
I said: I'll close any thought of you.
    She said: I'm a night rover; I traverse another path.
I said: The scent of your hair is a seducer of my life!
    She said: If you know it, it'll be your salvation
I said: The air filled with the morning breeze is pleasant.
    She said: Cool is the breeze blowing from the beloved's alley.
I said: The anticipation of drinking from your lips is lethal.
    She said: You accept slavery, the lover of slaves will come.
I said: When will your kind heart sue for peace?
    She said: Do not divulge the secret, until the time is ripe!
        I said: Did you notice how the time of pleasure ran?
        She said: Silence, Hafez: this tale, also will run.

Hundred and Forty-Four

As the east sun streams forth a cup of wine,
    a thousand tulips blossom in the garden of Saghi's face.
The breeze breaks the hair of hyacinth
    when from the meadow blows the scent of her hair.
The tale of the night of separation is not the story of *self*:
    even his short utterance amounts to a hundred epistles.
From the upside down table of the heavens expect little bounty;
    without weariness, a hundred woes fill a morsel!
You cannot reach the golden goals, relying on your works;
    the deed is not done without the hand of grace.
If patient, like Noah, in the face of the flood,
    calamity will cease and a thousand years[294] of life[295] will come.
        As the breeze of your tresses pass over the dust of Hafez,
        from the dust of his corpse a hundred thousand tulips rise.

Hundred and Forty-Five

It has been some time since you've favored us with news!
    Where is my confidant to send you messages?
We cannot hope to attain that high purpose
    unless your grace set a few steps in our direction.
When wine from vat to jug is drawn and flower sheds her veil,
    take a chance with pleasure, drink a few cups.
Mixed sugar and roses, no cure for our ailing heart:
    give us kisses, mixed with few insults.[296]
O pious man, pass from the alley of rendaan with caution
    to escape ruination from those infamous men.
You've denounced wine: now find a heart to praise it;
    for a time, do not negate wisdom in the hearts of other men.
You beggars of the tavern, only God is your aid;
    look not for reward from a bunch of asses!
How pretty did the Old Vintner tell his lees drinker,
    "Do not tell your heart's pain to untutored men."
        Hafez is on fire with the delight of the light of your face;
        For a time, you the successful, care for those who have failed.

Hundred and Forty-Six

Aazari[297] clouds churning, Norooz[298] breeze flowing:
    I demand my wine and musician, who claims the arrival.
Beautiful faces in sight, I, shamed by my empty purse:
    The burden of love in poverty is hard to bear!
Now a time for giving gifts, but face must be saved:
    pawning our garment, wine and flowers must be bought.
Perhaps, my luck will change, for at dawn
    I prayed as the morning was coming.
With a thousand peals of laughter, rose came to the garden:
    perhaps smelling the scent of a generous man in the corner!
A garment rent in the way of rendi, what of it?
    In the way of good name, a garment could also be rent.
Who else would utter the praises I've uttered of your ruby lips?
    Who would suffer the transgressions I've suffered from your hair,?
If the justice of Sultan would not inquire after the victims of love,
    all hopes of tranquility for the reclusive are for naught.
        I do not know who shot the killer arrow of love at Hafez;
        I know this much: his joyous verse is dripping with blood!

Hundred and Forty-Seven

Friends, remember your companion of night;
    remember the right of devoted worship.
When drunk from the lover's sighs and moaning,
    remember it to the melody of maracas and harp.
When the grace of wine glows on the face of Saghi,
    remember lovers with songs and hymns on their lips.
When in the midst of desire, hope avails,
    remember to bring up the promise of our talk!
When the steed of luck gallops unchecked for a time,
    remember companions with the tip of your riding whip![299]
When you do not grieve for those who are faithful,
    remember the perfidy of the wheel of fortune.
        A matter of kindness, you denizens of high places,
        remember Hafez's face and this threshold of his.

Hundred and Forty-Eight

Your delicious scent, whoever heard[300] it from the breeze,
  he heard from an intimate friend intimate expressions.
O king of beauty, cast a glance at the beggar:
  many tales have these ears heard of kings and beggars.
I tease with musk-scented wine my inner sense of scent, for
  I smell the scent of duplicity from the garment of the Sufi.
The secret of God the vested Gnostic refused to divulge,
  I'm in a shock: where did the wine-seller[301] hear such?
O God, where is the confidant of secrets, that for a time
  my heart may explain what was said and heard.
Undeserving, this loyal heart of mine
  verbally abused for my tenderest love.
If prevented from visiting your alley, what of it?
  Whoever heard the scent of faith from the garden of fate?
Come Saghi! Love is calling urgently.
  Any who told our story, he heard it from us!
Not just today we drink our wine under the cover: [302]
  the Master has heard this story a thousand times!
Not just today we drink wine with the song of harp.
  Many cycles the wheel has turned since hearing our song.
The advice of Sage is the essence of piety and source of joy;
  happy the person who listens to it with patience.
    Hafez, your duty is uttering prayers, that's all:
    never mind if He hears it—or not!

Hundred and Forty-Nine

You're the dawn, I'm the lonely candle of morning.
　　Smile at us and see our soul as we submit.
Since my heart is branded hot by your unruly tresses,
　　pansies will mourn over my dust—when I die.
I had pinned my hopes on the threshold of your door
　　to throw a glance at me: you threw me out of your sight!
How shall I thank you, you army of woes—God forgive you—
　　when at time of loneliness you remain in my mind.
I'm a slave to the pupil of your eye whose cruelty causes
　　a thousand drops of tears rain, as I count my heart's plights!
Our idol parades in many eyes, but
　　none sees this amorous wink that I glean from her eyes!
　　　　If like wind any passes by the dust of Hafez,
　　　　from that delight, in the narrow grave, he'll rend his shroud!

Hundred and Fifty

From fire in my heart, I boil like a fermenting vat;
    in a sealed vat, blood red juice seethes in silence, turning to wine.[303]
It's suicide to yearn for the lips of the lover.
    You observe me! I'm trying with all my heart![304]
When will I taste freedom from the pain of love, since
    every moment the locks of a new beauty enslave me.
God forbid! I'm not a believer in my own sense of worship:
    certainly I indulge in a cup of wine—from time to time!
I am hopeful, despite the enemy, in the day of judgment
    His gift of forgiveness will not burden me with sins!
My father[305] sold his share of Paradise for two kernels of wheat.
    Why can't I sell my share of this world for two grains of barley?
Wearing sackcloth is not a sign of overmuch conviction:
    it only covers a thousand hidden imperfections!
I want only to drink purified wine from the vat.
    No escaping, though: must listen to the Master's words!
        If musician thus tunes his music in love's praise,
        poems of Hafez will put me into a deep trance.

Hundred and Fifty-One

The veil on the beloved's face, the scourge of my life:
　glory the moment I can lift the veil from her face.
This cage unbefitting me, a person of beautiful melodies;
　I'll fly to the meadow in Paradise: I'm a bird of that garden.
It hasn't become clear yet: why I came and where I will go?
　How painful to admit I'm ignorant of the plans of fate!
How can I move to the space of the angelic world?
　In the scheme of being, I am tightly tied to my corpse!
If my heart's blood is scented with desire,
　no wonder! I and musk from Khotan[306] are co-aggrieved!
Do not judge me from the gold-threaded garment I wear:
　much hidden pain under this apparel!
　　Come! Remove the *self* of Hafez from his presence.
　　In spite of you, no one hears me, I am who I am!

Hundred and Fifty-Two

I'll never forsake my love—nor my Saghi:
  I've repented a hundred times; but not again!
The Garden of Eden, the shadow of Toobaa,[307] nor the palace of houri
  can ever compete with the dirt in the street of the friend.
Kerygmas and lessons of men of insight, only a hidden sign:
  I gave you a hint and will not repeat it again!
I've no sense of myself until
  I find my self in the tavern!
The know-it-all said with an acerbic taunt, "Abandon love!"
  No need fighting, Brother! I will not oblige!
Enough said of my piety: with the beautiful faces in the crowd
  I do not flirt from the top of a pulpit!
    Hafez, my Master, His Excellency is the source of fortune:
    I will not avert my eyes from the threshold of his door.

Hundred and Fifty-Three

With wicked black eye-lashes, you've bored a thousand holes in my faith:
    come, let me pick a thousand pains from your tippled eyes!
Oh, my heart's companion: have you forgotten your beloved?
    May I never sit a day without your name in my heart!
Senile, lacking reason, this world incites Farhaads[308] to shout:
    "Her deceits and spells have made me weary of my precious life!"
Like a rose, I'm soaked in sweat from this fire of separation.[309]
    O morning wind, blow my way a breeze to cool dry the sweat.[310]
The mortal world and the living, both ransom of the beloved and Saghi:
    I consider kingship of the universe only a parasite of love!
If the lover chooses another in my place, beloved rules!
    Shame if I choose my life over the beloved's!
Morning, and the nightingale shrieked, "Where are you, Saghi? Rise up!
    My head is bursting with the thought of dreams of night."
The night of my passing: I will ascend from my bed to the houris' palace
    if you're the candle by my head at the moment of passing.
        The story of my desires, registered in this letter,
        are without errors: it's Hafez who has inspired me!

Hundred and Fifty-Four

I see it now! It's expeditious to move
    to the tavern and live in peace.
Drink wine and divorce duplicitous folk:
    cut my ties from people of this world!
But for my wine and books, none my companion,
    to avoid chancing upon deceitful adversaries.
Like juniper, I rise free of people
    to say adieus to this world, when possible.
So often I've lied about truth in this soiled apparel,
    I'm ashamed of rosy wine and the face of Saghi—.
My heavy heart and the burden of beloved's love, alas,
    my poor heart is not—up to that!
If I'm a rend of the tavern, or the city's holy man,
    whatever you see in front of you: I'm less than that!
I'm a slave of Aasef,[311] don't mislead me:
    if I breath, he'll exact the price from the wheel!
        Much dust of cruelties in my heart; O God, do not allow
        the mirror of my love to become dulled in annoyance.

Hundred and Fifty-Five

Sorrows of life—I do not see an end to it—
    other remedy than ruby wine, I do not see!
I will not leave the service of my Master;
    I do not see any advantage in it.
From the sun, you measure the heights of pleasure:
    I do not see the luck of propitious time![312]
The sign of God's people is loving—keep it in mind:
    I do not see such a sign in the elders of our city!
To these two perplexed eyes of mine a thousand regrets:
    with the two mirrors, I see not the beloved's face.
As your stature grew from the rivers of my eyes,
    in place of juniper, all I see is running water.
In this withering mind, no one makes the gift of a draught.
    Observe! I cannot see a soul mate among this lot!
The token of the one to whom I offered my heart?
    Do not ask me! I cannot see *me* in the crowd.
      Except me and the skiff of Hafez in this sea,
    I cannot see any skill for singing beautiful verses.

Hundred and Fifty-Six

Happy the day I leave this ruinous home behind:
    seek comfort and go after beautiful faces.
Strange paths lead one nowhere; that I know well:
    I only traverse in hopes of the beloved's tousled hair!
Terrors of Sekandar's[313] prison lie heavy on my heart;
    I'll break my tent and move to the realm of Fars.[314]
Like the ailing breeze with impatient heart,
    I'll go for the love of that robust juniper.[315]
If destined to die on the way to my lover, I'll go as a reed[316]
    with a wounded heart and eyes crying with tear.
If released from my sorrows one day, I have vowed,
    I'll dance the way to tavern, singing ghazals.
For my beloved, humbly dancing
    will I go to the edge-well of the luminous sun.
Taazian[317] do not care for the people who are suffering?
    Paarsian,[318] you help to send me happily home!
      If like Hafez, I cannot escape the desert,
      I'll accompany the court of the Aasef[319] of time.

Hundred and Fifty-Seven

Sufi, come! Let's remove this garment of deceptions,
    cross out and cancel this picture of pretensions.
Oblations and building of new mosques, we promise!
    Garment of deceit we wash in the fountain of the tavern.[320]
On resurrection, if we're not allowed in Paradise,
    we'll steal young boys and the gathering of houris.
Tipsy and joyous, we rise, and from the feast of Sufis
    plunder their wine and embrace their beauties!
We'll feast, lest we're murdered with regret within us
    when this sack of bones we drag to another world!
The secrets of God, hidden behind the curtain from us:
    sufficiently drunk, we will unmask it!
Show me the brows of the beloved, so, like the new moon,
    we may drive the sky-ball with the bat of the beloved's curl.
        Hafez, it's not our place to boast so much.
        We should not overreach our short grasp.

Hundred and Fifty-Eight

Though servants of our king,
    we're the kings of the land of dawn:
treasures in pocket; purse, empty;
    in hand, the magic goblet,[321] but dirt of the floor;
aware of the present, drunk with pride;
    the sea of Toheed,[322] drowned in sin.
When lady luck flirts
    we're like moon, mirroring her face!
At night, to the fortunate king
    we are guardians of his crown and hat.
Say! Savor and value our conversation,
    for you're asleep and we are wide awake.
Shah Mansoor[323] is aware that
    we'll put forth all our honest effort:
we'll bloody the shroud of enemies;
    we'll bestow to friends robes of victory.
Not a grain of deceit in our nature;
    we're red lion and black viper!
        Tell them to return the debt to Hafez.
        You've confessed it, and we're witness to it!

Hundred and Fifty-Nine

Do you know what is the pleasure in seeing the rise of a friend?
    Preferring beggary in the lover's lane to accepting a crown!
To cut out any hope of living is easy to come, yet
    it's hard to cut out a dear friend from your life.
To the garden I come, like a blossom, wearied;
    there, in good reputation, will I rend my shirt:
At times, like the breeze to the rose I tell my secrets,
    at times, hear, from the nightingale, love-making songs.
You cannot neglect kissing the lips of your beloved, lest
    at last you become tired of biting your lips and hand!
Value the conversation of your friends: once,
    from this forked road we pass, there is no returning.
      Perhaps, Shah Yahyaa[324] has forgotten Hafez.
      O God, remind him to care for the Darvishes.

Hundred and Sixty

If knives rain in the house of my beauty
    I'll submit to it: it's God's command.
Tradition of virtue, we also knew,
    but what solace with misguided luck?
I do not know about sheikhs and preachers:
    either you serve wine, or shut up!
I'm a rend and a lover in the season of roses:
    God forbid if I repent at that time!
Your affection does not reflect a picture upon us:
    you, with the face of a mirror: alas your heart, alack!
Patience is bitter, life fleeting:
    I wish I knew the terms of our separation.
        Hafez, why this moaning if desiring union:
        you must eat your heart out, from time to time!

Hundred and Sixty-One

At down, I dragged myself to the tavern door, sleepy:
  the hem of my garment wet, prayer-rug, wine soaked.
Came Mogh-bacheh,[325] the wine-seller boy, regrets on his lips:
  He said: Wake up, you sleepy journeyer.
Wash-up first, then to the tavern you slink;
  so as to keep you from contaminating this monastery!
How long will you lust after the sweet lips of lads,
  contaminating the essence of your soul with ruby wine?
Pass your old mansion[326] in piety and avoid
  contaminating the honored robe of age, with a youth's habits.
Cleanse and become purified; escape the well of base being;
  water once contaminated by mud cannot be cleared.
I said: My Love, nothing is wrong with the lore of roses
  to contaminate spring with ruby wine!
Devotees of the path of love in this deep water were
  drowned yet never contaminated by water.
    "Peddle not your riddles and epigrams, Hafez," the boy protested.
    Alas this favor, contaminated with many angers![327]

Hundred and Sixty-Two

You, who have come with your long, wavy hair,
    God bless you: you've come to tend to the insane.
Set aside your coyness for a time: forget old habits:
    now, you've come to inquire after the needy one!
In front of your eyes, I'll die, peace or war,
    since you've come worthy of coyness and love!
You've mixed water and fire on your ruby lips;
    evil eye away! You've come with tricks!
I praise your soft heart for good deeds:
    you've tamed your coyness with the prayer of the dead?
How does my piety take it? To plunder my heart you've
    come to the cave of secrets, drunk and disheveled!
    "Your sack cloth is soaking with wine, Hafez," she said.
      "Have you forsaken the religion of this land?"

Hundred and Sixty-Three

Come, Saghi: the tulip cup over-flowing with wine:
    we'll know when the ultimate event,[328] and where false tales?
Let pride and coyness pass, for the world has seen
    the wrinkle in the robe of Caesar and the crown of Key![329]
Caution! Meadow birds are tippled—alas!
    Wake up: perpetual slumber in your pursuit, be aware!
Happily strutting with grace, O you new growth of spring:
    may you never suffer from the fury of Dey.[330]
Trusting neither the love nor motives of the wheel of fortune:
    Woe to anyone, who ever trusted its antics.
Tomorrow,[331] the wine of Kosar[332] and houris of paradise will be ours:
    today also, a beautiful Saghi and a cup of ruby wine!
The morning breeze from the time of foolish youth remembers
    an elixir that removes the grief of years from youth.
See the passing pomp and glory of the rose,
    each leaf trampled under the feet of the wind's valet.
Honor Haatameh Taa-ee[333] with a cup of wine, its weight, a mann[334]
    to end the cruel sins of jealous men!
From that wine, flushed purple on the face,
    bled out the favor of his nature from his face.[335]
Set your dais in the garden, where, as servants,
    junipers stand at attention and reed prepares.
        Hafez, the story of your magical charm has spread to
        the borders of Egypt and China, even cities of Rome and Rey!

Hundred and Sixty-Four

If, hearing the song of nightingale and dove, you refuse wine,
    how can I heal you?—Your affliction, beyond my craft!
Make provisions from the scents and sounds of spring time:
    for the bandits of Bahman and Dey[336] are in hot pursuit!
When flowers drop the veil—and birds cry,
    let not your cup drop: why cry, "Alas!—Alack!"?
Glory of kingship, beauty of a face—they've no permanence:
    only a word remains of the throne of Jam[337] and crown of Key[338]
To be the treasurer of inheritance-mongers is folly in the words of
    musicians and Saghi and the decree of tambourine and reed.
Fortune never gave without demanding it back:
    seek not compassion from this wicked world; she's worthless.
It is written on the columns in Paradise:[339]
    woe to him who bought worldly flirtations.
No more generosity, and I end my words: I say, where is my wine?
    Serve it for the gladness of the soul of Hatatameh Taa-ee.[340]
        The miser has never heard of God; come Hafez,
        take a cup and be generous; I guarantee that ruby!

Hundred and Sixty-Five

Life passed in lust and futility:
    You, boy, fetch me a cup of wine; may you live to an old age!
With what thanksgiving in this town they are contented—
    royal falcons of the truth—descending to the ranks of a fly!
Yesternight, as I followed among the army of her servants,
    She saw me and said, "Oh, you smitten lover! Who are you?"
Like a bag of musk, with his bloodied heart he must be happy[341]
    who is renowned to be connected to a musk-scented beauty.
A light blazed from Mount Sinai, and I discerned it rise:
    perhaps, an ember I can fetch for my friends![342]
The caravan has left; you, in deep sleep, the desert, ahead,
    alas! You're so ignorant of the tolling of those bells.
Open your wings; soar to the tree of life;[343]
    pity a bird like you, imprisoned in this cage.![344]
Like the scent from a censor, I'll cling to friends, who
    set the world afire with their scented breath.
        How long will Hafez have to seek to find you?
        May God enhance my efforts to catch up with you![345]

Hundred and Sixty-Six

New Spring, come: be blithe and happy:
    so many roses in bloom, you still stuck in the mud!
I will not advise you with whom to sit and what to drink:
    you will know it, if you are wise and clever.
The harp in secret gives you advice, but
    it will only benefit those who are worthy!
In the garden, each leaf a page from someone's book of ecstasy:
    a pity if you remain unread.
Excessive woes of this world will rob the cash of your life,
    if you keep this difficult story alive, day and night!
Although the road from us to our friend is danger filled,
    the going is easy, if you're aware of the stations!
        Hafez, if your good luck helps,
        you'll be the prey of that pleasant admirer.

Hundred and Sixty-Seven

A thousand tries to win you for my lover,
    fulfiller of the wishes of my restless heart;
to make you the eye-sight of my nocturnal life,
    a companion of my hopeful heart.
Since the kings of charm feign disdain to their slaves,
    in that crowd, you become my god.
That agate, your lips' coyness, the cause of my woes,
    to be my consoler if I complain of woes.
In that garden, where belles hold the lover's hand
    if you can, hold my hand and be my love!
Of a night, you come to the lover's cottage of sorrow:
    for a moment, be the companion of my mourning heart.
The graceful sun becomes my puny pray,
    only if a gazelle like you becomes my prey for a moment.
My wages to take three kisses from your two lips!
    If you refuse, you'll be forever in my debt!
I have a wish, that at mid-night
    instead of flowing tears, you sit by my side!
        Though Hafez[346] of this land, I'm worth only a whit
        unless, you with your grace, become my love!

Hundred and Sixty-Eight

This garment I wear, better in the pawn of wine;
   this mindless booklet,[347] better drowned in wine.
Since I wasted life—when I reexamine time:
   better in the corner of a tavern, tippled and gone.
Since rational rumination is far from darvishi,[348]
   better heart on fire and eyes full of water.
I will not speak about the condition of the ascetic to the people:
   if I ever tell this story, it better be with lyre and the violin.[349]
Since the affairs of the heavens are foul, from this side
   better lust for Saghi with wine in hand.
Such a lover as you: I'll never abandon;
   if I am to pull a burden, better the weight of your tresses.
      You are old, Hafez: leave the tavern;
      rendi and lusting best when you're young.

Hundred and Sixty-Nine

Who will bring from my lover a penned caressing?
    Where is the messenger of the breeze to afford us a grace?
I just did the comparison: the advice of reason in the way of love
    is like a single dew-drop, falling upon the body of an ocean!
Understand! Though my garment is the pawn of the tavern,
    from the wealth of endowment, you'll not see a sou in our name!
My heart, the tradition of disputes brings on a headache:
    take a cup and rest yourself for a time!
Ignorant healers will never know the pain of love:
    you, heart-dead, go seek a breath from Jesus.
I'm ashamed of deceit and the hidden secrets I keep:
    Better I fly a flag at the door of the tavern!
An opportunist will sell both worlds
    for a cup of pure wine and the company of a beauty.
Duration of pleasure—and wealth, not aspects of loving:
    if our companion, then drink the poison of woes.
I am not complaining, but the friend's mercy clouds
    have not rained in the fields of thirsty hearts!
What for! Why not buy for the price of a sugar cane?
    He has spread a thousand sugar motes with his reed![350]
        O King, reward of your worth is not in the hands of Hafez,
        except prayers at night and supplication in the morning.

Hundred and Seventy

Early morning, a wayfarer in a land
    was telling this enigma to his friend.
O Sufi, wine clears only
    when aged in a bottle for forty days.
God is weary a hundred times of a garment
    that in each sleeve a hundred idols hide.
Although generosity is a body-less name,
    it is you offering your need to a beauty!
O prosperous farmer, God reward you,
    if you reward a poor reaper.
I see no joy of pleasure on any face:
    no heart, soothing, no joy of religion!
Inside, pitch dark! May, a miracle
    light the chamber of the recluse!
If a ring is not of Solomon,[351]
    what use the design on its signet?
Although hot tempered, a tradition among the fair,
    what blessing if they soothe a grieving soul!
Show me the way to the tavern so I can ask
    about my end, as it is foretold!
        No spiritual private lessons for Hafez,
        nor absolute knowledge for the ascetic!

Hundred and Seventy-One

Return, Saghi: I'm intent on serving you;
　　anxious to be of use and praying for your success.
Since the grace of the cup's prosperity is your light,
　　show me a way out of the darkness of my bewilderment!
In the sea of sinfulness I'm drowned in a hundred ways:
　　acquainted with love, I'm among the graced.
Do not blame me for my rendi and infamy, O learned man:
　　this has been my appointed lot from the court of fate.
Drink your wine: falling in love is not our will or want;
　　this gift I received from the inheritance of my nature.
Not during my life have I chosen to journey from my home, but
　　for the love of seeing your face, I would journey to alien nations!
Deep sea and mountains on my path, and I, tired and weak:
　　O auspicious Khezr,[352] help me with my resolution.
My heart away from the doors of your mansion;
　　yet, soul and heart, I am a resident of your mien!
　　　Hafez will expire in front of your eyes.
　　　I'm of this mind; let life afford me this respite!

Hundred and Seventy-Two

But for the love of beauties, my heart chooses not just any path.
  I offer *it* advice from many directions: the heart refuses.
For God's sake, O giver of advice; speak of jug and wine:
  not a clearer picture in our mind, more pleasant than wine.
Come, beautiful Saghi, bring the ruby wine:
  not a clearer thought inside us, better than wine.
I carry the jug up my sleeve, and the folks think it my books.
  It's a miracle the blaze of this lie set not my own book[353] afire.
One day, I will burn this ragged, patch-work garment of mine, for
  even the old vintner refuses to exchange it for a cup of wine!
No wonder friends show such fondness for ruby wine:
  except for truth, there is no elemental design in its nature.
Such eyes and beauteous form, and you ask me to leave my lover!
  Leave! This nonsensical preaching will never overcome my power!
The advice-giver of rendaan, who quarrels with kismet:
  I see him so wearied; does he not indulge in wine?
Midst weeping, I cry: like a candle in this gathering:
  I have my igneous tongue, but it doesn't catch on fire!
So propitious, hunting my heart! I adore your tippled eyes:
  no hunter has ever hunted wild birds better!
The point is our need and—the disdain of the lover:
  what gain using spell, if it doesn't work on that beautiful face?
I'll find that mirror, like Alexander:
  no matter if there is wine in it or not![354]
God's mercy, O man of treasurers: Darvish of your alley
  knows no other door—nor another path.
    In spite of his fluently sweet verses, I'm baffled by our King:
    why is Hafez not clad in garments of gold?

Hundred and Seventy-Three

Her black her, such complaints have I: do not ask why!
    I'm totally discomposed by her: do not ask why!
May no one refute his heart and religion, hoping for faith:
    I am so remorseful of my deed: do not ask why!
Just a draught! That doesn't hurt any one.
    I suffer such blames from the ignorant: do not ask why.
Preachers, pass us by in peace, for this ruby wine
    thus steals the heart and religion: do not ask why.
What gossips on this path burn the heart,
    bellowing, "Do not see this; do not ask why."
Virtue and health were my aims, but
    such flirtations from those seductive eyes: do not ask why!
I thought: I'll ask after the arch of the wheel: hello!
    It said, "I suffer under the bat so much: do not ask why."[355]
        I asked, "For whose blood have you fixed your hair?"
        Reply: "Hafez, it's a long story; by Koran, do not ask why!"

Hundred and Seventy-Four

What need my garden of juniper or pine:
    our home boxwood is no less precious!
O handsome lad,[356] what of this religion you profess?
    Our blood is more kosher than the milk of a mother!
Detecting the mist of chimera from a distance, ask for wine:
    we've examined the wine; the cure is at hand!
Why turn away from the Master's threshold?
    Our fortune is in that house, and the answer at his door.
The woes of love, nothing but a fable, yet—this a wonder:
    there is no repetition, from whatever tongue I hear the word!
Yesternight, he promised consummation, but he was wined in the head:
    we'll see what he says and what today is in his mind!
Shiraz[357] and Roknee[358] brook, and this perfumed breeze:
    find no fault in it, it bears the mole of the seven lands![359]
A difference in the Water of Life, flowing from its mysterious source,
    and our brook, its source from the Allah-o-Akbar Pass![360]
We'll not dishonor poverty—or blame prudence:
    tell the king, we're well set— and happily fulfilled!
        Hafez, what a rare sweetness your pen runs:
        its fruit, more pleasant than nectar and sugar.

Hundred and Seventy-Five

Wine is refreshing, breeze scented with the rose, beware:
    do not drink wine to the music of harp, the bailiff[361] is on the prowl!
If you happen to hold on to a beauty—and a jug,
    drink wisely; seditious are the times!
Hide your jug under the sleeve of your tattered coat:
    like the eye of the jug,[362] times are bloody!
With tears, we wash our coat clean of wine;
    it's time for self-restraint and piety!
Seek not solace from the revolving dome; its nature, contrary:
    this arched horizon is brimming with impure affliction!
The ascending firmament is a bloody sifter, the smallest bits through it:
    the head of Kasraa[363] and the crown of Parveez.[364]

      Hafez, you've conquered Iraq and Fars with your sweet verses;
      come now, it's the Baghdad's turn and the time of Tabriz.[365]

Hundred and Seventy-Six

Now that the rose holds a cup of clear wine in hand,
    nightingale sings the rose's praise in a thousand tongues.
Take a book of verses and follow the path to the fields:
    not an occasion to visit the school or discuss Kashfeh Kashshaaf![366]
Yesterday, our tipsy jurisconsult gave an official decree:
    henceforth wine is unkosher, only the title of the Foundation![367]
You've no choice between clear wine or one with lees:
    whatever our Saghi picks—we imbibe it!
Forget about the people, and like the phoenix take a measure:
    the fame of a hermit goes from Gaaf to Gaaf.[368]
The tale of the rivals and the thoughts of companions
    Are storied by the gold embroiderer and the mat weaver![369]
      Silence, Hafez, and keep your red-gold witty words:
    the banker in our town is a forger!

Hundred and Seventy-Seven

Did you see it? The friend had no intention but cruelty and oppression:
    broken promises and no sorrow for our woes!
O God, do not punish our lover, although our heart of a dove
    the lover broke and killed and did not keep the hunter's law.[370]
To us, unfaithfulness was ordained by our lot; otherwise, our friend,
    far from it, only lacked a tradition of grace and love.
All said, any who did not suffer our lover's abjection,
    wherever he went, he did not see honors.
Saghi, fetch the wine and tell our sheriff
    not to deny us, for such a cup even Jam did not own.
A wayfarer whose path did not lead to the door of the lover
    is a poor messenger in a desert, forbidden to enter holy places.
      Hafez, glory in your fluent words, for the rival
      has no art and is unaware of it!

Hundred and Seventy-Eight

Saghi, bring the wine, the month of fasting is gone:
    fetch me the jug; the season of chastity and fame is gone!
Much precious time wasted: we must make amends
    for the life wasted sans our jug and a cup of wine.
Make me so drunk that I no longer recall
    who has been here and who has gone!
In hopes a draught will reach our lips from your cup,
    we have prayed for you, day and night, from that bench.[371]
A heart, thought dead, receives a new life
    when the pleasing scent of wine touches his nose!
Of his vanity, the ascetic failed to come to a good end,
    and the rend, of need, ended up in the Garden!
Whatever cash in my heart, I spent it on wine.
    The transaction feigned: the reason for the taboo!
In your fire, how long can I bear to burn like incense:
    bring me wine, for my life is spent on vain transactions!
    Enough advising Hafez: it's no use!
    A lost soul who's tasted of the delight of wine!

Hundred and Seventy-Nine

Come Saghi, the lover has lifted her veil:
    the lamp in hermit's intimate circle is re-lit.
That briefed candle is glowing now;
    this ancient man, reclaiming a new youth.
This one with her flirtations misled the Mufti;
    that one graced a friend, so his enemy ran.
Wonderful your sweet, luscious witty words,
    as if your pistachio[372] coated words with sugar.
Over the burden of sorrow in our wearied heart,
    God sent Jesus-breath, and we were healed.
The belles who vied with the moon and the sun in beauty,
    on your arrival, left for a different duty!
The seven domes of Heaven are retelling this story:
    what shortsightedness to pay it no heed!
        Hafez, who taught you these words that destiny
        made an amulet of your poems and covered it with gold?

Hundred and Eighty

O Lord, so ordain that my friend safely
  come to rescue me from the bondage of censor.
Bring the dust from the path of my traveling friend
  to make the friend's residence the center of my discernment.
Alas, my path is blocked from six directions:[373]
  mole, lines, hair, face, cheek, and stature!
Today, I'm in your presence: offer me your favor;
  tomorrow, when I'm dust, what benefit tears and regrets?
You, who chatter about love with your allusions and words,
  we've no words for you—of grace or health!
Darvish, do not complain of the sword of lovers:
  this tribe demands damage from the murdered man!
Burn your sackcloth, for the arch of Saghi's brows
  breaks a corner of the prayer altar of Imam![374]
God forbid if I complain of your cruelty and deceit:
  the injustice of lovers is all gifts and favors.
      Hafez will not cease to sing the story of your locks:
      these stories continue till the resurrection day.

Hundred and Eighty-One

The scent of your curls, keeps me tippled for good,
    the magic in your eyes holds me forever drunk.
After all this patience, O Lord, will I see
    the candle in my eyes light the altar of your eyebrows?
I hold dear the pupil of your eyes, for
    in my soul it has etched a copy of your Indian mole![375]
Desiring to adorn this eternal world fully,
    better tell Zephyr to lift your veil for awhile!
If longing to defeat the legacy of death from this world,
    open up, scatter a thousand lives from each strand of your hair!
I and Zephyr, two beggars, wandering and idle,
    I, drunk with the spell of eyes; wind, with the scent of your hair.
      Hafez deals well with this world and the other:
      nothing is worth to him more—than the dust of your lane.

Hundred and Eighty-Two

Wine and secret love, both just a fancy:
   we've entered the ranks of rendi, come what may!
Open up your heart and mention not the heavens above,
   the calculation of no engineer can solve this enigma!
Let not the sedition of times bewilder you, for the wheel
   remembers such tales in the thousand thousands!
Friend, hold the jug with respect and deference, for its composition
   is from the head-skull of Jamsheed and Bahman and Ghobaad![376]
Who knows where Kavoos and Key have gone?
   Who can guess how Jam's throne was lost?[377]
I still see: from the desire for the lips of Sheereen
   tulips grow from the blood of the eyes of Farhaad![378]
Did the tulip know the perfidy of the wheel, so
   from birth to becoming, never put down the cup of wine?
Come and notice, and let's drown in wine for a time:
   perhaps we'll come in this ruination to a house of treasures!
They do not grant me permission to travel and enjoy
   the scent of the breeze and the waters of Roknaabaad!
      Without the sound of harp, like Hafez, take not a cup:
      happy hearts are wrapped in the silk-strings of harp.

Hundred and Eighty-Three

Old age, and I'm dreaming of a young lover!
    The secret I hid so well is public now!
Just in my mind, the bird of my heart sails in the air.
    O sight, look and see into whose trap it fell!
Alas, because of that black-eyed musk deer,
    like a bag of musk, my heart is torn, bleeding!
It was from the dust of the passage in your lane
    that bags of musk fell into the hands of the breeze!
Your eye-lashes, when they held the conquering sword:
    how many live-hearted dead look at each other?
Much experience we have from this world of woes:
    whoever argued with lees drinkers, forfeited!
No matter how diligent a piece of granite, it won't turn to a gem:
    what can it do with its ill begotten nature?
        Hafez, who trifled with the hair of idols,
        now has met his terrible match in his idol![379]

Sufi set his traps and opened his magical ware:
    a partner with the trickery of the firmament.
The plays of the wheel brought him to shame:
    he was offering falsity to the people of perception!
Saghi see! The vain witness of Sufis
    has come to display—flirting has begun.
Whence come this musician, who makes such araagh[380]
    then returns his tune to the gates of hejaaz?[381]
My heart, come, and let's seek God's protection
    from those who wear short sleeves and have long arms![382]
Do not affect, for any who loses his love in guile
    to him the meaning of love remains a puzzle!
When resurrection is at hand, ultimate truth will become apparent:
    woe to the man who has worked only in metaphors.[383]
You, happy quail, where are you hurrying—tarry a while:
    do not be fooled by the cat at prayer!
        Hafez, do not blame rendaan, for in eternity
        God releases us from any need of the deceitful ascetic.

Hundred and Eighty-Five

One cannot touch that ringlet of your parted hair
    and depend on your promise, nor that of the breeze!
I'll try my best to claim you, yet
    at times, we cannot change our fate.
Great pains when we succeed holding on to a friend;
    alas, the chains of perfidy will not easily unclasp!
The face, it cannot be compared to the moon of the heavens:
    appellation of "a friend" cannot be assigned to just any jack!
When my slender beloved rises to sammaa[384]
    what worth my life—if I cannot offer him that?
A cleansed vision can discern the face of God:
    nothing reflects on a mirror with a film of dust.
Insight into Love is out of the realm of our gnosis;
    trying to solve the enigma with rational thought, a lapse.
Flooded by jealousy, knowing you're the beloved of many, but
    I cannot fight, day and night, with the creatures of God!
What can I say? You're of such a sensitive nature
    I cannot say much, but whisper a prayer!
      But for your arched brows, Hafez has no altar;
      obeying anyone —but you—is not in our religion!

Hundred and Eighty-Six

Did you see, my heart, what mischief again the woes of love wrought?
    Sooner the sweetheart, what the lover did with the faithful love?
Alas, those bewitching eyes, what a turmoil they incited?
    Alack, the tippled man: how he behaved towards temperate men!
My tears, colored aurora because of the lover's indifference:
    look at my lackluster luck, how it affected the matter!
At dawn, lightning flashed from Leili's dwelling:
    pity what it did to the harvest[385] of the heartbroken Majnoon,.[386]
O Saghi, pour the wine, for the invisible Author
    will not tell what He does behind the veil.
He who designed this azured circle:
    no one could discern what he did in the motion of His circles.
      The thought of love set afire Hafez's heart—and burned.
      See what an Old Friend did to His old friend!

Hundred and Eighty-Seven

You'll only have a look at the secrets of Jam's cup
    when you medicate your sight with the dust of the tavern.
Never without wine, and musician under the dome of the wheel:
    to the tune of this hymn, you'll cleanse your heart from your pain.
The flower of your desire will remove her veil
    only when you offer your services—like Zephyr.
Begging at the doors of the tavern is a potent remedy:
    if successful, you'll transform dirt into gold—alchemy.
Set a first step forth with the intention of loving:
    much profit in such a long traveled roving.
You never leave the mansion of your natural self![387]
    How will you happen at the door of the conditions of Life?
The beauty of the friend is not veiled:
    let the dust settle before looking deep again.
The elegance of presence and order in life
    can only be achieved by the grace of a discerning man.
But you, desiring the beloved's lips and your draught of wine
    cannot hope to achieve another task.
My love, if you acquire knowledge of the guidance light[388]
    like a candle, laughing, you will be happy to lose your head!
        Hafez, if you only listen to this regal admonition,
            you'll start in the path to your transcendent destination.

Hundred and Eighty-Eight

If I dare to leave, the lover will cause a riot;
    if I sit with desire, rancor will rise!
And if, as if a wayfarer, out of loyalty,
    like dust I fall in front, like wind she flees!
If I beg for a slight kiss, a thousand regrets
    fall from her deceitful lips like sugar bits.
That deceit I detect in your eyes
    will mix my flood of tears with the dirt of road![389]
The landscape of love's valley is filled with many mishaps:
    find me the lion-hearted—who doesn't fear any haps?
You're patient, in love with life, but this imposter wheel
    has a thousand more new tricks than this!
        Yield your head in resignation, Hafez, for
        if you're harsh, with you life will be even harsher.

Hundred and Eighty-Nine

The treasure of Sufi is not all pure and guileless:
    heaven knows how many sackcloths deserve setting afire!
Our Sufi, who got drunk on morning prayers,
    at night—never worry—he will be drunk with wine!
Happy the day to bring the touchstone to rest;
    to shame him who is false in the test.[390]
If Saghi's hand draws such designs on the water,[391]
    alas, many faces will be painted in blood.
Those pampered in luxury cannot take to a friend:
    love being the arena of the afflicted rendaan.
How long will you suffer the woes of this world? have wine;
    a pity if a knowing heart remains troubled.
        The garment and prayer rug of Hafez, the tavern will take;
        if the wine is served from the palms of a beautiful mate!

Hundred and Ninety

How can a flowing ghazal inspire, if the mind is saddened?
  We hinted at the point, and that will be that!
From your ruby lips, if I receive the pardon-ring[392]
  the thousand riches of Solomon I will find under that seal.
My heart, we cannot grieve for the reproach of envious men:
  perhaps, when reconsidered, you'll find your grace in that.
Anyone who cannot fathom this fanciful pen,
  even an artist from China is revealed as an imposter.
A cup of wine or sorrows, each to a different man:
  in the circle of the events, conditions vary.
About roses and rosewater, this is the final verdict:
  this, a witness in the bazaar; that, a denizen of the veil.
    It's not that Hafez has forgotten rendi:
    the former remains till the day of the latter.[393]

Hundred and Ninety-One

The breath of Zephyr will scatter the scent of musk:
  when the old returns—again to become young!
Red bud will offer a ruby cup to jessamine;
  the eyes of jonquil will look anxiously at peony.
The assaulted nightingale suffers for separation pains;
  to the court of the rose, bellowing he will run!
From the mosque to tavern, if I move, no blame:
  the convention of preaching is long, and time is flying!
My heart, if postponing today's pleasures to morrow,
  is there surety for the permanence of life tomorrow?
In the month of Shabaan,[394] do not stop drinking, for this sun
  will disappear until the eve of the feast of Ramazaan!
The rose is dearest, enjoy its company now, for
  it came to the garden from this door, soon leaving from the other!
Musician, a feast is for hymning and singing ghazals:
  what of this talk of who left and what will happen?
    For you, Hafez came to the realm of existence:
    set a forward step to greet it; it's on the way to exit!

Hundred and Ninety-Two

I'll never forget the love of black-eyed beauties:
    my destiny and theirs, intermixed.
Our rival has annoyed us much, no room for peace:
    the sigh of the early-risers will not flow to heavens.
In creation I was not ordained to be any, but a rend:
    whatever portion ours—will never be rescinded!
O God, bailiff, forgive us for the noise of our tambourines and reeds:
    the canon laws will never be voided because of our deed!
My solution is to make love to my beloved in my mind:
    what shall I say of embraces and kisses that never come?
Ruby wine and a secure place and a caring lover, Saghi:
    O Heart, when will you be fulfilled, if not now?
      Do not wash, O eyes, the print of woes from the chest of Hafez:
      it's a wound from the sword of his lover; it will not heal.

Hundred and Ninety-Three

The day of separation and the night of absence from beloved have ended:
    a good omen I say, the star of luck swept and the matter is ended.
All the flirtation and frills that autumn commanded
    finally at the feet of the spring breeze they ended.
Thanks be God: with the coming of the vision of rose
    the conceit of Dey-gales[395] and glory of thorn[396] are ended.
The dawn of hope, that mystical veil of those who retire to pray:
    tell them to come out; the darkness of their night has ended.
All those worries of nights and the woes of heart:
    under the shadow of the beloved's hair are ended.
I cannot still believe the perfidy of our times, yet
    the tale of woes, because of the beloved, has ended.
Saghi, thanks for your favor; may your jug always remain filled with wine;
    for your prudence, the worry of not being drunk has ended.
        Although no one counted Hafez much, praise God,
        all that boundless burden and reckoning has ended.

Hundred and Ninety-Four

A star gleamed, the source-light moon of the convention,
　　becoming friend and companion to our bewildered heart.
My lover, who never was schooled and never writ a line,
　　became with flirtation the teacher of many teachers.
In hopes of their darling, the heartsick lovers, like Zephyr,
　　became the ransom of jonquil's face and the eyes of narcissus.
Now, my friend seats me at the head of the table;
　　behold the beggar of the city, who became the darling of the party.
He who dreamed of the water of life—and the cup of Alexander
　　became a drinker to the health of Sultan Abulfavaares.[397]
The pleasure-house of love will now flourish, for
　　the arch of the beloved's brows has become its architect.
Wipe from your lips the taste of wine, for God's sake:
　　my mind by a thousand sins becomes diverted!
Your flirtations served lovers such a wine
　　that the world lost its wits, and wisdom became fatuous!
Like gold, my poems are kept dear—granted:
　　acceptance of discerning men becoming the alchemy of this copper!
　　　From the road to tavern turn your reins, for
　　　Hafez went this road and became a beggar!

Hundred and Ninety-Five

Zephyr comes in praise of the Old Vintner, for
    the season of joy and pleasure, flirtation and drinking come.
The weather, like the breath of Jesus; and the wind, spreading musk;
    the tree has donned a green garment, the bird coming to a song.
The fire of tulip, the wind of Spring fanned so much,
    brings blossom to a sweat and flower to a boil![398]
With your wit, do listen to me—try delectation;
    this word, at dawn, I heard from invisible voices.
Leave any thought of dispersion, becoming whole:
    as when Ahriman left, came Soroosh.[399]
I cannot fathom what the lily heard from the morning bird[400]
    to silenc the tongue of wine.
The assembly of lovers is no place for the words of invaders;
    cover the jug: the wearer of sackcloth rushing, on his way!
      From the mosque Hafez is heading to the tavern.
      Has he sobered from the wine of deceit of piety?

Hundred and Ninety-Six

A greeting, like the scent of a lover,
    to those people with discerning eyes.
A praise, like the light of the pious,
    to that candle of secluded piety.
I cannot see a single friend in place:
    I grieve: where are you, Saghi?
turn not away from the alley of the tavern;
    a key is sold here to unlock all doors.
The bride, this world, though in her ultimate beauty,
    will push, alas, the limits of perfidy!
My wounded heart, if it has any self respect,
    will never seek healing from those heartless men.
Sufi-effective wine, where is it sold?
    I seek cure from deceitful piety!
Friends broke our promise of friendship
    as if there had never been friendship!
If you'll let me, my greedy self,
    I'll rule as a king in my beggary!
You'll be taught the alchemy of happiness
    when from a bad company you're parting!
        Hafez, do not complain of the cruelty of life.
        What do you know, O creature, of the plans of the Creator?

Hundred and Ninety-Seven

I have a pact with my friend, as I live,
    I'll treat his admirers in the alley as myself.
I'll seek from Chegel[401] candle my private, generous heart:
    from Khotan moon, the glint of eyes and the light in my heart.[402]
Since with the pleasure and desires of heart I have found intimacy,
    what care have I of the malicious talk in the assembly?
At home I have a juniper, in whose tall shadow
    I've no need of a wild cedar, nor boxwood in the meadow.
If a hundred armies of beauties march to steal my heart,
    thanks to God, at home I have an army-thrashing beauty!
It merits for the lover's ruby ring to boast "I'm Solomon."[403]
    Where Great God is, what fear of Ahriman?
O Wise Ancient, find no faults with our tavern; yet
    forsaking wine, I am inclined to break such a promise.
God! O Rival, tonight close your eyes for a time
    so I can talk with the lover's silent rubies in secret!
Sauntering in the garden of my lover's luck—praise be God,
    I have no desire of tulips or narcissus—nor a taste for roses.
      Hafez is famous for his rendi among companions, but
      no regrets: I have Ghavaam Al-Deen Hassan[404] in my domain.

Hundred and Ninety-Eight

Last night, in a flood of tears from my eyes, I was wakeful,
    on the surface of the flowing water, drawing your face.
The brow of the friend in my mind, and the sackcloth on fire,
    I drank a cup of wine in memory of my altar, your eyes.
The lover's face just in front of my eyes appearing;
    from a distance: I only kiss the face of the light of moon!
My eyes fixed on Saghi, my ears to the sound of harp,
    I find an omen, by sight and sound, in this case.
The picture of your face, until the morning came,
    I kept in my eyes, in insomnia wide awake!
Saghi pours wine to the music of this ghazal of mine:
    I sing this hymn and drink from that clear wine.
      Hafez has good times; and the omen, just right:
      I drink to life and the health of my friends.

Hundred and Ninety-Nine

Good tidings, my heart: a Jesus-breath is on his way:
    from his happy soul, the scent of someone is coming.
Do not moan for the woes of separation, for at dawn
    I saw an omen: a redeemer is coming.
From the fire of the desert of Ayman,[405] I'm not the only happy man:
    there, in hopes of catching on fire, Moses is coming.
No one I know who doesn't have some business in your alley!
    Anyone there, for a fancy—or whim—they are coming!
No one knows where to find the beloved's dwelling;
    I know this much: for certain, the sound of bells is coming.
If a friend despairs for the illness of a friend,
    tell him to be happy: his breath still is coming!
Ask we of the nightingale of this garden,
    "I hear the moaning of a bird from a cage coming!"
        Friends, my friend has in mind to annoy Hafez:
        to hunt a mere fly, Phoenix coming!

Two Hundred

If with the musk-laced wine my heart is killed, perhaps
    the scent of charity does not come from false piety!
If the whole world denies me love,
    I will do whatever God has ordained.
Do not give up your hopes in the grace of miracles, for
    charitable men forgive sins and reward lovers.
My heart resides in the circle of our talk, hoping
    to open a curl from the hair of the beloved.
You, blessed with beauty and luck,
    what need of a beautician?[406]
Meadow is beautiful, air, clear, and wine, pure:
    now, but for pleasure, nothing is allowed.
Beautiful is the bride of the world, but beware:
    this chaste woman will never marry any soul!
I told the tulip, "O beauty, what will happen
    if, for the token of your thanks, a tired man rests?"
        With a smile, the lover said, "Hafez, don't ask God,
        for your kiss may taint the moon!"

Two Hundred and One

If wine will not the woes of our heart take away,
 the fear of the event our roots will take away!
If drunkenness will throw anchor,
 how will the ship from this abyss of calamity get away?
Alas, with everyone the wheel wins in absentia,
 and no one in this game can win a hand away.
Our passage is set in darkness. Where is the path of Khezr?[407]
 God forbid that the fire of dispossession take our honor away!
My ailing heart is allured by the meadow
 to rescue my dying body: the Zephyr will take the illness away!
I am the healer of love, pour the wine, for this elixir
 brings peace of mind and takes vile thought away.
  Hafez burned, and no one told his lover
  unless a breeze, O God, should take the message.

Two Hundred and Two

Now the scent of Paradise scatters from the meadow:
  I, the pleasure of wine, and an angelic mate.
Why not boast the beggar of his wealth?
  Cloud-shadow is his royal tent, meadow's edge banqueting hall.
The meadow whispers stories of the month of Ordibehesht:[408]
  it's not so wise to buy on credit and pay in cash!
Delight your heart with wine, for this ruinous world
  is intent to make mud-bricks from your dust.
Seek not faith from an enemy who is unenlightened:
  it's a candle lit in the monk's cell from the flame of a pagan temple.
When I'm to be buried, blame me not for drinking wine:
  well aware I am of what the destiny has wrought.
      Do not sulk at Hafez's funeral, for
      although drowning in sin, to Paradise he lights.

NOTES TO THE POEMS

[1] See note 70.

[2] "naa-" is generally a sign of negation, literally meaning, "he is no Dervish at all." However, the implication is that anyone who lays claim to be a Darvish, is a false prophet.

[3] Hafez uses "osprey." In traditional Persian mythology, osprey takes bones to the top of a mountain and chews on them, instead of hunting for fresh game, a vulture-like quality, unbecoming the majesty of the bird.

[4] In the manner of a dervish, under the condition of being a dervish.

[5] In Islam, blood is considered impure and non-sacred. Since wine is also impure, the juxtaposition of the two words creates a tension: If I have desecrated the temple with my blood, then you desecrate my body before funeral with wine, a condition that well suits the poet.

[6] I have translated the Persian word "zaahed" as "ascetic." Both in English and in Persian the state of virtue is desired, but in Hafez those who pretend to virtue mistake the appearances with the truth. These false ascetic are unfriendly, unloving, negative, and self righteous. Hafez uses "zaahed" as an anomaly

[7] The word is "meykhaaneh," literally a tavern. However, Hafez juxtaposes tavern with such words as mosque, school, place of worship, all holders of negative charge. Thus, the deep meaning of the word takes the place of the truth that a mosque or a place of worship should have, but does not.

[8] Hafez uses "khodforoosh," on one level referring to those who are ostentatious. However, I think a stronger word, "prostitute" is implied

[9] "Sedreh" and "toobaa" or "toobee" refer to the "tree of life" in The Garden of Eden, shading the devout and the angels. The tree is visible only to God. I have translated the two as "tree of paradise."

[10] Reference is to Jacob, the father of Joseph, whose elemental metaphor has been used by Hafez in a number of his ghazals. Of course, through the ghazal he alludes to the separation of the father from his son for many decades and the hardships of Joseph in Egypt, each line making a different kind of reference to the notion of separation. The story in the Koran is much more elaborate than in the Old Testament, and the sentiment of separation is more profoundly felt.

[11] Hafez uses "rezaa," an honorific level of mystical achievement, where yielding is the order of being, not self will.

[12] The term "peereh dehghaan," meaning "the old farmer," is also used to refer to aged wine as a personification. Perhaps, this is also a reference to Ferdowsi, the Old Master of the Iranian epic poetry.

[13] A Pseudo-Quranic verse tells the story of Solomon, whose air-borne chariot made noises. An ant on the ground alerted the rest to hide. Solomon, on hearing the ant, asked the reason for hiding. The ant replied, "You are in the air, and I on the ground, but there is no depending on earthly affairs. My fear is that your end would be mine if your time has come!" The allusion is to the temporary nature of life, even for such a person as Solomon, God's prophet (anointed king) on earth.

[14] This ghazal offers some of the most exquisite poetical music in Hafez through the use of alliterations. Unfortunately, a reproduction of such musical effects is impossible when translating from Persian to English. Just for a taste, I include here the first line of the poem:

> *jaan bee jamaal eh jaanaan meyleh jahaan nadaarad*
> *har kas keh in nadaarad haghaa keh aan nadaarad.*

You may notice the repetition of the sounds /j/, /m/, /a/, /aa/, which provide the music for the poem.

[15] In the first half of this line the reference to the "bent harp," an ancient Persian musical instrument, is balanced in the second half with an admonition: "Listen ! The advice of the aged will not hurt you." The aged "harp" and "aged" advice giver become one and the same. I have chosen to alter the words for the sake of this translation.

[16] Considered the most mystical of Hafez's poetry, this ghazal proposes that God's true nature is love, and out of that love he created the universe. Human love reflects this divine love so that a man and a woman in love reproduce, in minuscule degrees, that love which fashioned chronos from kyros. I think there is an interesting parallel here between what Hafez says and the theory of the Big Bang. See also note 140.

[17] The complicated passage proposes that out of the divine love, when we aim low, God's grace moves us to a higher plain of being.

[18] This ghazal is considered one of the most mystical poems of Hafez. The light from God emanates and dazzles the man into ecstasy of recognition; once thus glorified, an inner light flickers and takes the initiate into a higher understanding of creation.

[19] Except for rare occasions, Hafez uses the word "Sufi" derogatorily to mean a superficial, pretentious man, who has little interest in the matters of spirit, but a great deal on what the title will bring him.

[20] I have translated "mohtaseb" as a jailer or a gestapo, or a heretic. The connotation of "police" does not make a strong enough point.

[21] "Zonaar," a cummerbund worn by the Eastern Nestorian Christians by the order of the Moslem rulers to distinguish them from the Moslems: a worthless piece of cloth.

[22] "Riyaa" and "saaloos," vaguely meaning "hypocrisy" and "flattery," are considered two of the most major sins in Islam.

[23] Hafez says, "Hypocrites and flatterers cannot become Moslems." I have chosen "grace" to make the context more universal.

[24] I have generally used Hafez's Persian word "saaghi" as "muse" in other ghazals. However, I felt the emphasis should be on the Cup-Bearer, thus deviating from my original plan.

[25] I have translated "gheyrat" as distraught, which is not exactly its meaning. The English word "Jealousy" simply does not convey the meaning that Hafez desires. However, in other instances, when context permits, I have used "jealousy" directly.

[26] Hafez uses the Arabic word "sedreh," twice used in the Holy Quran. It refers to a tree in Paradise, large and heavenly, seen only by God. I have translated it as "Tree of Life," for a lack of a better word. In the Old Testament, Book of Genesis, several references could be found about the tree: 1) The Tree of Knowledge of Good and Evil, from which Adam and Eve ate and as a result were expelled from the Garden of Eden, and the Tree of Life, which was, after the expulsion, guarded by two angels with swords of fire. Man has no access to this tree any more because the promise of eternal life has been taken away by God.

[27] Although neither Quran nor the Old Testament makes any mention of a Solomonic ring, in the apocrypha a story is told about a signet that Solomon wore. On it the name of the Almighty had been inscribed, and the source of Solomon's authority was that ring, which surpassed all the other authorities on the earth. Thus, in this metaphor the reference is to the power of the ultimate, and the beloved of the first two lines alludes to God.

[28] The Old Testament Fruit of Knowledge of Good and Evil is identified as an apple tree. In the Isalmic tradition it is either grapes or, more commonly, wheat. The cause of the expulsion--beyond theological speculations about the nature of Man-- was eating wheat. The reference here is just to that plus the aesthetic Iranian metaphor of "wheat skinned," literally, "olive skinned" beloved is considered beautiful and desirable, thus a double entendre here to reflect both of these references.

[29] Referring to the miraculous healing powers of Christ.

[30] Perhaps the reference is to Sultan Gheyaath Aldeen Mohammad Shah II of Delhi, a patron of the Persian Language and Literature, who invited Hafez to visit India.

[31] A wealthy financier and the chief tax collector, who was also a patron of Hafez, supporting him both financially and artistically.

[32] Hafez uses "blue" and "green" alternatively for the color of the sky and the sea. I suspect the elevation and the dust in the atmosphere changes the color from blue to bluish green.

[33] Two famous mythological kings of the Keyaan Dynasty.

[34] A tragic Persian and Arabic legend, close to Romeo and Juliet, Leili and Majnoon, two members of the same tribe, grew up together and finally fell in love. Majnoon's father would not consent to their marriage, and the lovers die of heart break. I have reversed the order of the original Persian half lines for grammatical considerations.

[35] In the Islamic tradition, some slaves who reached an old age, were freed out of respect to their longevity. Freeing any slave was considered a great act of godliness, rewarded by a promise of Paradise.

[36] Those who sought justice wore paper garments as a symbol and appeared before a judge for restitution.

[37] A classical love story, in the tradition of Tristram and Isolde and Romeo and Juliet, where Farhaad, a stone carver, falls in love with Shereen, the beloved of King Khosro Parveez. The king banishes Farhaad to the mountains, forcing him to cut stones for his palace. When false news arrives that Shereen has committed suicide, Farhad throws himself from the top of the mountain to his death. It is said the mountains still echo the shouting of Farhaad.

[38] This is an elegy written on the occasion of the death of his son. Here, Hafez is personified by "nightingale" and the child by "flower."

[39] One of the attributes of "peereh moghaan" is "beloved." Other synonyms are love, rend, master, over soul, and many others. This word always stands in contrast with "moamen," "zaahed," words meaning virtuous, which have negative connotations for Hafez.

[40] The term Hafez uses is "Parveen," which is translated as Pleiades, a word most unpoetic. I chose "stars" instead to get around the antiseptic connotation of the English word.

[41] The reference here is to God: God is the ultimate ruler.

[42] See note 37.

[43] In the creed of most Sufis acceptance and suffering are great virtues. It is similar to the Christian notion of turning the other cheek. In the literary tradition that Hafez is following, overlooking imperfection and forgiveness are supreme virtues, so that in this poem and others, Hafez professes to being maligned, but not caring about it. The tradition proposes that the people of God are always maligned, very much what Christ tells his disciples that they will suffer in his name and that the cross will be carried by those closest to God. The philosophical term in Persian for this schools of thought—and behavior—is called "malaamati," literally, accepting blame without protestations.

[44] Here Hafez uses the word "khod parasti," which is roughly "egotism." I think "self-indulgence" gives a better flavor of Hafez's intentions if one considers the poem in totality.

[45] See note 37.

[46] Perhaps a reference to Khaajeh Jalaal Al-deen Touraan-Shah, Vazeer of Shah Shojaa, and a major patron of Hafez. Himself a mystic, Khaajeh supported poets and mystics.

[47] Because of translation complexities, I have slightly varied the text. The original should read, "without your face, o juniper tree, any beauty (gol andaam) is illegal!"

[48] The word "mohtaseb" translates to "policeman, agent of a government, a morals police," which cannot work in an English context. I have translated it as "judge," "bailiff," or "sheriff."

[49] In Persian mythology pearls are formed by the drops of rain water in the mouth of a mother of pearl. The drop eventually is transforms into a priceless pearl.

[50] Hafez uses the term "khataa," which both means "an error" and also "China." In the light of the following verses, the word should be translated as China, but that would not mean much in English. So I have translated the word as "mistake," but the intention becomes clear in the next three lines.

[51] Khotan, famous for its musk, is a city in Turkistan, now a part of China.

[52] In traditional Persian poetry, especially that of the Sufis, nightingale represents three qualities: 1) ecstasy and a lover's fever, 2) eloquence in expression, and 3) angelic voice, often invoking frivolity.

[53] In Islamic tradition the myth goes that Noah carried Adam's corpse on his ship in order to control the gale if it got out of hand. Perhaps the "clump of dust" is a reference to the body of Adam.

[54] The allusion here is to Joseph of the Old Testament, who went from prison to the Lordship of Egypt.

[55] The word used is "van yakaat," a reference to a verse in Quran, often recited to ward off evil eyes. The whole verse reads, "The heathens nearly cast their evils eyes upon you [Mohammad] when they heard Quran and declared you mad."

[56] As in Greek Mythology, in the Persian tradition Venus represents frivolous love and treachery while Mars represent wars and cruelty. In effect, the verse is questioning both pleasure and pain as meaningful affects of this life.

[57] Bahraam, also known as Bahraam eh Goor, a Sassanid king of the ancient Iran. He was fond of hunting onager, or "goor," thus the appellation "Bahraameh Goor." There is a double entendre here: "goor" also means grave, so that the second part of the verse could be read as "no sign of Bahraam or his grave." Both have disappeared from the face of the earth.

[58] See note 13.

[59] "Morning Breeze," as I have translated Hafez's "Sabaa," reputedly is mild and often hesitant. It moves, then lingers, blows then is quiet, like an ill person who has to stop often to catch his breath. In the Persian literary tradition, "Sabaa" is called the weak and ill wind!

[60] The Moslem Shrine towards which the faithful turn to pray and make pilgrimage.

[61] Reference to the House of Jacob.

[62] Reference to Joseph of Old Testament and Quran.

[63] In effect, he who is born is doomed to die; there is no escaping this final fate.

[64] Persian myth suggests that, in the heart of the sun (albeit, sun's rays), stones change into garnets, rubies, and other precious stones. This verse says, "I have achieved much spiritual eminence as my treasure trophy; how can I look at the treasure being created in the heart of the sun?"

[65] Quran promises Moslems the reward of the Paradise and a river that runs through it, River Kosar. What flows through it is "Sweeter than honey, whiter than milk, colder than snow, and softer than cream."

[66] The Persian text reads, "King of beauties, Khosro of Shereen mouthed." Both double entendres, "Khosro" refers both to any sovereign and also the specific King Khosro, as "Shereen" refers to "sweetness" as well as the beloved of Khosro. There is no possibility of showing these parallel textual structures in English. The closest example in English would be the first two stanzas of T. S. Eliot's "The Love Song of J. Alfred Prufrock." The "yellow fog" refers to the literal fog that envelops the building as well as the mist colored cat that circles the house and curls into itself to rest. Persian poetry uses such devices in abundance because the language allows the poet to be multi-layered.

[67] Perhaps "subject" is a better word, but "slaves" makes the point more readily.

[68] Reference to God.

[69] I have a suspicion that this half verse could also read," Avoid the company of those who break their cups."

[70] Until the time of Hafez, the word *rend* (-*aan,* plural) characterized a person with low morality and of the lowest cast in the society, the butt of the jokes of the higher, refined, spiritual and intellectual superiors. Hafez switches the meaning and applies a "rend" to a person who is irreverent and a free-thinker. He is irreligious but has a great sense of the divine. He is gruff and irrational outwardly, but filled with sensitivity and kindness inside. He disparages the cleric, but he has a sense of the presence of God. If the cleric are hypocritical, he is an honest man. A libertine and an honest man, trustworthy. The "rend" possesses equilibrium and lives according to the golden mean. This juxtaposition provides Hafez with an even sharper tongue to criticize the ruling caste of his society on their own terms.

[71] Similar to *rend*, a lowly person who has the heart of a lion.

[72] I have translated the Persian word "ragheeb" as Master. Traditionally it has meant a protector, a presence, working as one's conscience, an inner voice of reason. In later years it came to mean two or more people vying for the love of the same beloved, a competitor.

[73] I have translated words such as "naazaneen" as "beauty."

[74] God, the Creator, the Designer of life.

[75] A virtuous cleric, who fell under the spell of a Christian woman and forsook his followers; then, with the intervention of Prophet Muhammad, he was restored to virtue. The woman also repented and became a Moslem. The point is that, if you are a true lover, do not fear infamy: eventually all will come right!

[76] The term refers to one of the highest degrees of spirituality, where appearnces of religion are torn and the person lives a Godly life despite the appearance of being a heretic.

[77] See note 21.

[78] "Tasbeeh" refers to the idea of remembering God with sincerity and purity.

[79] The quotation is from Arabic, which interprets the first half of the verse: Hafez is sitting by the palace of the beloved, nymph-natured, pines, and tears flow from his eyes like streams from the side of a hill in a garden [Garden of Eden?]. There are Quranic allusions in the statement.

[80] Hafez uses the word "haraam" in "...cho man zinjaa begzaram haraamat baad...," but I could not find an English word to replace it. Such words as "illegitimate, unlawful, religiously prohibitive" simply do not work in translation.

[81] See note 13. The implication is that the prayers of those virtuous men who are "vigilant at night" brought about the miracles ascribed to the signet.

[82] See note 13.

[83] In literary tradition, the metaphor of bow and arrow refers to eye-brow and lashes. Obviously, Iranians do have thick eye-brows, connected in center, giving the shape of a bow. I will venture a guess that this is not so with most of the Germanic people. So, there is a naturalness about the metaphor of bow and arrow for Persians.

[84] Two of Shah Shojaa's viziers were patrons of Hafez. The first one was Ghavaam Al Din Mohammad, and the second, Turaan Shah, to whom the poem is referring.

[85] A cup bearer; I have used the word Saghi when I have felt Hafez really means a cup-bearer. More often, however, I have used "muse" to refer to this word. It seems that in most cases Hafez is using muse of inspiration, both spiritual and psychological by this word.

[86] Potiphar's wife, who, according to the Quran, tried to seduce Joseph [also in Hebrew Scriptures].

[87] Ghazal is a short, lyrical Persian poem, similar to sonnet, but not structurally as formalized. The length of a ghazal can vary from five to fifteen lines with varying metrics and scales.

[88] Life is short and fleeting, the wheel of fortune running its course.

[89] The reference is to wine.

[90] See note 265.

[91] A cup, a mirror, with ability to reveal the secrets of the universe, a sort of magician's globe in which one can see what is happening in the universe. Ferdowsee, the great epic poet of Iran, talks of the mythological king of Iran, Key-khosro, who possessed the cup and could see the events in it. In the Persian Folklore, the cup is used to symbolize our universal yearning to know the secrets to which we have no access. Persian mythology credits Alexander the Great with the invention of mirror.

[92] A reference to Darius III, an ancient king of Persia.

[93] I have used Khanlari's version in this line.

[94] See note 76.

[95] Reference of Baayazeed Bestaami, one of the greatest mystics of the Islamic world in Iran (circa ninth century).

[96] According to the Quran and Old Testament, Moses and God made a covenant on the Mount Sinai for the Jews to become God's chosen people in return for God's blessing. This verse is an allusion to that event, which asserts that, with the covenant, Moses is confident of hastening to meet God in the right place and right time.

[97] The Day of Judgment.

[98] I have translated "vaght," "time" as "moment." In mystical language "time" refers to a moment when a person is freed from time and all that the ticking of the clock accrues a person, gaining insight, which timeless.

[99] The term used here is "mohemmaat," I presume meaning matters of importance. I have used "cognition" to relay the idea.

[100] I assume "peymaaneh" means both "a measurement" and also a "cup." I chose the first meaning, aware that perhaps this is a double entendre. It could be translated as, "They kneaded Adam's mud and molded it into a cup."

[101] This reference comes from a Quranic verse, where no one is willing to shoulder the burden of the "trust" except the ignorant human being. I am at a loss concerning the nature of the trust, but I assume it could be "human nature," "soul of man," or "the burden of cognition." A suggestion is made by Shariar Zangeneh that "trust" in the Sufi lexicon means "love."

[102] An Islamic tradition suggests that the whole world will divide into seventy-two nations, eventually one becoming righteous and saved; the remaining will burn in the fire of hell.

[103] Here the word used by Hafez is "parvaaneh" or butterfly. In English, butterfly does not work, and I have chosen "moth" in its place.

[104] See note 223.

[105] In the Persian marriage tradition, this is "marriage portion," a sum agreed upon ahead of time, but payable to the bride after the wedding, if she demands it; perhaps a dowry.

[106] The first month of the Persian calendar, the first day of which is the first day of spring, often March 21.

[107] A vizier of Shah Shojaa, a patron of Hafez.

[108] Azure blue is the symbolic color of the Sufis; they often wear garments in that color.

[109] Here knowledge is "mystical knowledge." Hafez says, "We will not write sophistic ideas in the book of knowledge," referring to the canon of mystical knowledge.

[110] The term Hafez uses is "laaf," roughly boasting, bragging. However, keeping with the lexicon of Hafez, I believe "declaring" is more appropriate.

[111] Again, Hafez uses, "peereh mey froosh," akin to "peereh moghaan," and others. So for consistency, I have kept the term "Master" for all these variations of the same concept.

[112] Ibid.

[113] The word used is "messtabeh," a kind of balcony or platform erected insides a tavern, where the dignitaries sat and watched. A place of honor.

[114] Here Hafez uses the word "soosan," meaning iris. Traditionally the iris plant remains green year-round, and for that reason poetically it is used to indicate freedom, free to be green as it pleases. The flower also represent an articulate self, for it expresses itself perennially in its green covering. The metaphor could not work in English, so I have used an English idiom.

[115] A province in southern Iran, the capital of which is Shiraz, the beloved hometown of Hafez.

[116] Reference is to Jajaal Al Din Tooraan Shah, the last vizier of Shah Shojaa, a patron of Hafez. The name is mentioned in the following line.

[117] The line in Persian reads, "Those who turn dirt into alchemy with their gaze." This structure does not make sense in English, so I have substituted the phrase "…change lead to gold."

[118] See note 70.

[119] The word Hafez uses is "enaayat," literally "a favor." In the Sufi lexicon the word is used to refer to the paradox of yes and no, whether man has freedom of will or he is subject to predestination. I have used St. Paul's opinion that man's salvation comes from the grace of God, and not from "works," thus using the term "grace" for "enaayat."

[120] In the previous line Hafez leaves all matters in the hands of "grace"; however, in this line he admonishes the reader to accept what fate doles out, yet use his own initiative. This is the essence of "enaayat," determinism of life and the possibility of choice of the individual.

[121] Now there is a separation between man and his creator, and human life is ruled by much deceit and sedition because of man's arrogance. Hafez ponders, "What will happened when the curtain lifts?"

[122] A Quranic allusion, a shirt, soaked with the sweat of Joseph, was being carried to Jacob to cure his blindness, but the poet fears that the brothers might just have shredded it before it reached Jacob.

[123] The word "wise" can equally work in this line.

[124] The word Hafez uses is "sabaa" or "baadeh sabaa," which can be translated as "zephyr"; however, I find this word too harsh for the delicate music of Hafez, and often I have translated it as "morning breeze," unless the context definitely dictates otherwise.

[125] In the Quranic tradition Khezr is a companion of Moses, full of tricks. He has a special position with Sufis, equal to "Peereh Moghaan" or Master, as I have translated it.

[126] A reference to God. Mirror traditionally—East and West—reflects the human soul, which comes from God. Eyes are mirrors also.

[127] Narcissus is used to refer to the competitor of the beloved's eyes. The tradition also holds that the flower has eyes, but not sight, thus a deceptive appearance.

[128] The "candle" is the beloved, who weeps as it burns, telling the story of her diminishing for the lover. Butterfly, the lover, is too busy burning in the flame of the beloved to be aware of the story itself.

[129] Hafez uses "sahi baalaa-ee," or a tall juniper, which does not work in English.

[130] "If what Hafez practices passes for Islam, woe if there is a hereafter." In this ghazal, as in several others, Hafez uses a narrative style to escape sanctions by the over-zealous cleric. In Islam a narrative of "blasphemy" is not a blasphemy. This trick is similar to putting words into the mouths of animals—bestiary—such as in Chaucer's *Parliament of The Fowls* or the Indo-Persian *Kalileh va Damneh*.

[131] Mount Sinai, where Moses and God had an encounter. The desert, of course, refers to the path Moses and his followers took to cross to the promised land. In the poem, Hafez is asking impatiently when his encounter with God will arrive and when he will see the fire, indicating God's presence.

[132] Blame is a philosophical term for Sufis, who assume that "blaming" purifies love. I gather blame is akin to C.G. Jung's idea of individuation and awareness. By being open to blame, one comes to consciousness.

[133] Paradox, but hardly contradiction. The speaker simply assumes that human reason can go mad, very much as a human being can go mad.

[134] This line of Hafez is considered the most enigmatic and problematic writing of the master. No one has offered a convincing explanation of the line. My translation is based on a general understanding of what Hafez has said in many of his other ghazals. A literal translation is "Stop the adventure, and come again, for the pupil of my eye lifted the garment from me and burned it with thanks."

[135] Both the perfume and woad have their properties not because of their nature, but because the beloved uses them. Their essence is from the quality of the beloved's nature.

[136] Hafez says, "The balcony of the sight [vision] of my eyes is your nest." I find this too complicated a metaphor to use in English. So, I have simplified it in my translation.

[137] Here, Hafez uses "aaref," or gnostic.

[138] Powdered ruby in medieval Iranian medicine, mixed with other potions, was considered a curative for melancholy and sadness. One of its properties was to cause exhilaration.

[139] Hafez is impatient with the nouveau riche: I have slightly altered the wording to make sense in English.

[140] Sufi tradition holds that only human beings are capable of love, thus God's grace. Angels are incapable of such and must pay obeisance to man by praying at his door steps.

[141] Hafez uses "moghbachegaan," meaning young Zoroastrian boys who work in a tavern as cup-bearers. Yet, eventually, this word means Saghi, which I normally have translated as "muse," but here I assume it should remain as a physical cup-bearer.

[142] Sufi tradition routinely supports the idea of cutting the hair as a sign of mourning. The idea repeats itself in the following line.

[143] With the closing of the taverns, music is also silenced, and the harp moans the death by sheering its metaphoric hair!

[144] See note 21.

[145] Amir Mobaarez Al-Din, the father of Shah Shojaa, had put a ban on taverns and drinking. The poem is probably a complaint against those restrictions.

[146] Any wealth, not just the knowledge preserved in books.

[147] "je ne sais quoi," of French; that "indescribable quality and beauty."

[148] The second half of the line reads, "This is said by some one who has foresight in the art of roving eye."

[149] Compare this line with the following lines from John Donne's "A Valediction Forbidding Mourning" (1572-1632):

> *If they be two, they are two so*
> *As stiff twin compasses are two.*
> *Thy soul, the fixed foot, makes no show*
> *To move, but doth, if the other do.*

[150] Perhaps "amalee" should be translated as "compose," but I have opted for "sings" to justify the second half of the line for the English speakers.

[151] The use of the phrase "peereh golrang" is variously interpreted as "peereh moghaan" or "wine." I have chosen "rosy Master" to give the indication of the Persian "peer" as well as showing the contrast of the colors.

[152] The holy men of some Sufi sects wore green (azure) colored attire to distinguish themselves, an act for which Hafez had no room. He considered it an ostentation.

[153] The literal translation of the line is "from the outer (malak) to the inner (mala-kootash). The veil rises for whoever serves jaame jahaan nomaa (heart or wine). I had to work around this ambiguity, but the translation reflects the idea sufficiently.

[154] Norooz is the beginning of the Iranian New Year, literally "a new day."

[155] Hafez uses "feeroozi" and "behroozi," meaning "victory" and "prosperity," not strickly exact translations in English.

[156] A better, prosaic translation would be "Like a flower, abandon your blossom," a reference to the power of transformation: a flower cannot be unless it out grows the state of being a blossom. We cannot be what we are unless we give up what we had.

[157] Tending only to intellect at the expense of pleasure is foolish; the fools enjoy life; why not the wise?

[158] Quranic tradition suggests that Aasef was a counselor of King Solomon. By analogy, Hafez refers to all of his patrons in the court as Aasef. In this case, the allusion is to Viziers Shah Sheikh Abdul Al-Eshaag and Shah Shojaa, counselors to Turaan Shah.

[159] See above.

[160] I have taken a great deal of liberty with these lines. I am indebted to Shahriar Zangeneh for the meaning of this line, although he does not believe they belong to Hafez. I have included the lines because my main text edition, Khorramshahi, has included them in his version.

[161] Hafez uses "jelveh gaah," literally a bridal chamber.

[162] Capable of being self aware or oblivious, two states of consciousness that are paradoxical but can be available simultaneously for those who are among the initiate.

[163] Jam or Jamsheed is a mythological king of Iran, a member of Peeshdaadi Dynasty. Kaavoos Key is another mythological Iranian king.

[164] Letters outlining one's sins and transgressions. A record of one's life and deeds.

[165] I have translate the word "homaa" as phoenix. Homaa is the legendary mythical and mystical bird of the Iranian people. The bird was the source of good luck and prosperity. According to the legend, he on whom the bird casts its shadow, would be the king.

[166] Khorramshahi suggests that "we" is a reference to "human kind," "this place" to "state of being," "evil event" to Adam's disobedience and the fall, "path of love" to the underlying element of creation." I have translated "adam" as "not being."

[167] Perhaps a reference to the forbidden fruit. Hafez uses "mehre-geeyaah," meaning Belladonna.

[168] See note 164.

[169] Any number of fragrant substances mixed with wine to enhance its taste, bouquet, and potency.

[170] See note 158.

[171] See note 34.

[172] Persian poetic tradition compares the arched brows of a beloved with a bow and eye's lashes with arrows. So that, a look from the beloved is like being hit by "love" arrows (lashes) shot from the bow (brows); very much like Cupid's arrows, except that the Iranian tradition uses metaphor rather than myth.

[173] Literally, "The Way." The way of mystical attainment, one of the degrees of the ascending order in Sufism to reach as high as possible for the knowledge of God.

[174] Hafez uses the word "tagvaa." This is one of the seven levels of attainment in Sufism. I have used "piety" for lack of a more precise word in English.

[175] Perhaps Hafez's word "raah-ro" could be translated as "pilgrim," but I think of a pilgrim as someone who has an immediate destination; Hafez's "journeyer" has to pass seven levels of pilgrimage before arriving at the "Beloved."

[176] Hafez uses "hundred," but the common English expression is "thousand." I have used "thousand" whenever Hafez has used "hundred."

[177] Hafez uses two philosophical terms "dor" and "tasalsol." At the end of this line. I have translated them "cycle" and infinite. The proposition is that two objects cannot be the cause of each other except to affect a third object. "Tasalsol" does that reciprocally and infinitely where as "dor" is finite. The translation of this concept with a few words in a line of poetry is impossible, so I have simply hinted at the proposition.

[178] Hafez uses the expression "raxt be daryaa fekanash," or throw the clothes in the sea. The lexical meaning of the expression is "poverty stricken, become a beggar, a loser."

[179] Hafez uses the word "naa mahram" for which there is no equivalent word in English. I have tried such words as "non-initiate," "stranger," and such, but none works in English.

[180] See note 158.

[181] Hafez uses the word "bahr," "ocean" to contrast in the second half of the line with "ghatreh," "a drop." I had to find substitutes for these words to make the English translation idiomatic. Otherwise, the line would read, "The thought of an ocean's patience is impossible, far from it---what is on the head of this drop of impossible thoughts!"

[182] See note 125.

[183] The word Hafez uses is "bedaan kamar," which means "that belt" or "cummer-bund," or "waist," which does not make sense in English, and I have used "that high" to indicate the object is out of the reach of "any beggar." Perhaps Hafez means "embracing" the "waist" of the beloved, bought by the unbounded treasures of Gharoon.

[184] These are the five qualities of wine, enumerated by Hafez in this line.

[185] Reference to a small portion of food taken after drinking wine: a morsel. Of course, in English "chaser" is another kind of liquid drink that is taken after drinking an alcoholic drink. The Persian word is probably "mazeh," a word not found in English. I have substituted "chaser" for "mazeh," which is referred to in the word "noglash" at the beginning of the second half of the line.

[186] The beloved's lips.

[187] See note 31.

[188] See note 26.

[189] A reference to the Brook of Kosar (kothar?) which is located in the Garden of Eden; in it runs water which is "sweeter than honey, whiter than milk, cooler than snow, and softer than cream," due the faithful who enter the Garden. The source is the "Sureh of Kosar" in the Holy Quran.

[190] The first letter of the Persian alphabet is "alef," represented by a short, straight, vertical stroke. The figure of a woman is compared to that letter to show perfection of stance and carriage.

[191] Hafez uses "mobaarakbaadam," "my congratulations." It does not make sense in English, so I have substituted "pleasure."

[192] The Persian word is "Morghe Soleymaan" or "hod-hod."

[193] Hafez's word is "Saaheb deevaan," equivalent of the Chancellor of Exchequer in England.

[194] Hafez uses the expression "taht- o-fogh," or "head and feet" (tail), approximately meaning "oblivious."

[195] The half line reads, "har chand kincheneen shodam va aanchenaan shodam," which is not translatable into English. I suppose Hafez is developing a cause and effect relationship between his going to the tavern and his becoming inebriated; or, in mystical terms, through wine (the beloved) he comes to embrace the grace of God.

[196] Hafez uses the word "aakhare zamaan," meaning the last days of the universe before the day of resurrection. The Christian concepts "Parousia" and "Apocalypse," both will work here; however, the former is closer to the idea of Hafez, albeit a Christian idea.

[197] Hafez plays with words in this line, juxtaposing "year" with "month." The speaker is full of years, but the "half friend moon" is faithless. To be accurate as well as idiomatic, I have substituted the phrase "and the beloved, want of faith."

[198] Reference to the day when God made his covenant with Man.

[199] Here the Persian expression "saaz o sooz" is used, which means "bad and good," or "accept and live," and such. I had to alter it for the sake of the allusion to "candle" in the following half-line.

[200] Perhaps an allusion to the position of the Master, who is so elevated in stature that his umbrella is high beyond the skies.

[201] The word used by Hafez is "kasmeh" which is cutting a long bank of hair and curving it from center toward one ear, so that "breaking" it would mean tousling.

[202] I am translating the word "robaab" as viol.

[203] A reference to the Dome of Heavens and here, perhaps, a reference to "fortune" and "destiny."

[204] A petty king during the time of Hafez, who ruled for a short period of time in Shiraz and Esfahan. Hafez mentions him with affection.

[205] The original word is "arsh," or "throne."

[206] A vernacular expression such as "I swear to you" or "I swear on my honor."

[207] See note 158.

[208] See also note 13. Here Hafez uses the name Jam—a reference to the mythical Persian king—instead of Solomon. He uses the two names interchangeably.

[209] The false dawn before the true morning brings the day light.

[210] See note 163.

[211] This poem is one of the most satirical ghazals of Hafez, in which he makes light of all manner of social, political, and ecclesiastic foibles. Starting the line, "I have decided to repent and I told myself I must make an 'estekhare'," which I have translated as "magician," Hafez goes on poking fun.

[212] Hafez uses the words "togh," and "yaareh" meaning necklace and bracelet. I think my translation, although not literal, conveys his intentions.

[213] See note 89.

[214] Other words could substitute for "beauty," such as "virtue," or "absolute truth."

[215] In most cases, Hafez uses the word "Sufi" derogatorily"; however, in this instance he is using the word to indicate respect for a true mystic and a holy man.

[216] This is a reference to the sun.

[217] See note 116.

[218] Hafez uses the word "shagaayegh," or anemone peony. I have substituted the word "flowers."

[219] Hafez uses the word "Homaay," or "phoenix" to indicate the height of fortune that may come to anyone who beholds the bird.

[220] Hafez uses the word "baam" "roof." I have changed the word, although the meaning remains constant.

[221] The word is "bezan faali," or "faal begeer." I cannot think of an equivalent word in English, so I have chosen the word "lot" to convey the idea. Perhaps "taking a reading" might do.

[222] Hafez uses "saed-o-nahs," and then the names of the stars corresponding to good or bad omen, namely, Venus and Saturn. I have simply used the words "heavenly stars."

[223] Sheerin, a Princess of Armenia, beloved of Khosro Parveez, one of the kings of the ancient Sassanid Dynasty. Farhaad, a young man, also falls in love with Sheerin but pays for it by being consigned to the mines in the mountains to quarry stones for building the castle of the king. The love triangle is an old Persian story and an example of unrequited love. Sheerin also means "sweetness," often associated with the metaphor for fulfilled love. So the first half of the line could also be read as, "Much rewards will accrue you, O king of sweet mouths...."

[224] Essentially, the line says that unless you come to the singularity of the notion of God, you will not have grace within you.

[225] See note 46.

[226] The word is "soroosh" or "haatef," meaning an angelic voice bringing good tidings.

[227] In a number of poems Hafez juxtaposes those who drink uncleared wine (lees drinkers) and those who drink purified, filtered wine. Here I am using "cleared" to mean strained or filtered wine as opposed those people who cannot afford good wine and are "dordi kesh."

[228] There is no such word in English, but there is now. The beauty of English is in its versatility to accommodate all situations by allowing a writer to coin his own words, thus "sackclothed" from "sackcloth."

[229] The words Hafez uses are particularly cultural. "Deedeh mashoogheh baaz" is almost untranslatable into English. "Roving eyes," "Don Juan," "love addict," none will do, although all of these are a part of the phrase.

[230] Obviously, the reference is to the sliver of the moon seen at the beginning of the lunar month. The arch of the brow of the beloved seems to look like the new moon.

[231] Persian poetic tradition assumes that the heart of a lover nests in the hair of the beloved, thus the real home of his heart is the locks of the beloved.

[232] Perhaps the poems means to establish a metaphor of love, proposing that you cannot hope to go to the war of love with wisdom (reason), because—the beloved adds—my musk-scented hair is so strongly perfumed that the perfume of your wisdom pails in comparison and does not "worth a whit."

[233] Seeyaamak, the son of the mythical ancient Persaian King Keyomars, was killed by the Deeve (giant). Zoo is a mythical ancient Persian king, who was appointed to reign when he was very old.

[234] The Quranic tradition holds that God created Adam as His companion and made him superior to all the others of His creation, including the angels. Thus, angels prostrated themselves in front of Adam as a sign of Adam's superior position with God. Satan is a created angel, who refused to humble himself in front of Adam and was banished.

[235] See note 62.

[236] Hafez uses the word "kaar-khaaneh," meaning either a place of work or "this world."

[237] The Zoroastrian equivalent of evil or Satan. I have kept the original word for the sake of the unity of the ghazal. The poem was perhaps written to give heart to the people of Fars, who feared an imminent attack by Tamburlaine (Teymooreh Langh). God will not abandoned the people of Faars at such a time of need.

[238] One of the triad gods of Hindus, who reigned along with Vishnu and Shiva.

[239] In Persian, "khaandan" refers both to "reading" and also to "singing." Hafez's double edged use of the word cannot be translated into English, although one can justify "sing" because of a reference to musical modes and measures in the next half-line.

[240] In addition to referring to the Middle Persian Language, "Pahlavi" is also a musical mode and measure of ancient Persian compositions.

[241] Obviously the reference is to the Burning Bush in Quran and the Old Testament, where God appears to Moses in the form of a burning bush, all consuming and all light. The "rose" in the line perhaps could be best translated as "rose bush," but Hafez uses only "gol," meaning a "rose."

[242] Hafez.

[243] Here "Pahlavi" refers to a form of ghazal with a couplet rhyming scheme.

[244] See note 92.

[245] The implication is that, the breath of Jesus is healing and has the power of restoration to life from death. Thus, it is a strange story that "Our beloved killed us with the breaths of Jesus." This is a contrast for effect, not exactly an oxymoron, but a proposition that, if one is true, the other cannot be.

[246] "Molavi" is a special turban worn by the Dervish as a sign of distinction.

[247] Perhaps on the mystical level this is a reference to God and Christ, considered the Son of God by the Christians (God the Father and God the Son).

[248] Hafez writes, "You must become the dirt of the threshold of the learned men," which is too cumbersome in English. I have substituted "servant" for "the dirt of the threshold."

[249] In traditional Persian poetry, a lover's heart has two homes where the lover is fulfilled: the well on the chin and locks of hair.

[250] Hafez writes, "if you return still thirsty from the animal springs," which makes perfect sense in Persian but is rough in English. I have changed the word to "...the spring of this earth." A better expression would be "the well spring of life."

[251] See note 62.

[252] Refers to enlightenment, wine being the elixer.

[253] A special hat, filled with cotton, worn by Sufis; it is called "The Crown of Sufi."

[254] "Ghalandar" is similar to "rend," but a higher degree of achievement. See also 76.

[255] Tradition holds that the learned and the artist are usually the outcast of the society and lack station in the world.

[256] Hafez uses the traditional phrase "cheshm bedoor," which roughly means "God protect me from evil eyes." Some people are believed to possess evil eyes; a look may, even inadvertently, cast an evil omen upon the one who is the subject of the look.

[257] Persian literary tradition considers nightingale and rose complementary. The Nightingale goes mad with love when the season of rose arrives; thus, there is a lover's relationship between the two, and, symbolically, between human lovers and the spring time. One wonders if the genesis of giving red roses to a beloved might not be Persia and Hafez, a delicious proposition!

[258] See note 65.

[259] Traditionally, "jonquil" (narcissus) is a symbol of the beloved's eyes.

[260] Of the three varieties, Indian hyacinth is the most fragrant and beautiful. The color tends blackish, and in traditional poetry it symbolizes the hair of the beloved. Here, "two hyacinths" refers to the two strands of hair, one left, one right.

[261] Here, the word "aafi-yat," "well being" does not refer to health or physical security. The reference is to a state of spiritual and mental health.

[262] In poetic tradition, violet is used to personify a lover, who bends the head earthward, grieving over the absent beloved.

[263] Unlike such words as "zaahed," and sufi," the words "darvish," and "aaref" are terms of honor and truth. They represent the real mystical state that the former only pretend to possess. So, Hafez often speaks of a "darvish" with love and affection, perhaps considering himself as one of them. A point of interest is that often "darvish" and "sufi" are used interchangeably, but the difference is in the conditions of living, the simplicity of the Darvish versus the complexity of the Sufi ideal.

[264] Hafez uses "rezvaan" or "the gate-keeper" of the Garden of Eden. I have used the Old Testament term "seraphim."

[265] In other places I have identified "Gharoon" with the Greek "Midas" for the sake of convenience. In this verse, however, there are implications that require the use of the exact word. Gharoon, in Islamic tradition, was a man who amassed tremendous quantities of gold, too greedy to share with anyone. God became angry and one day caused the earth to open up and swallow the man and his treasure. As an added punishment, Gharoon is perpetually sinking in the darkness of hell.

[266] See note 158.

[267] See note 65.

[268] This ghazal is one of the pure love songs of Hafez.

[269] The three adjectival phrases could not be translated into English without sounding silly. "Shah-vash" is something like "face of a king or a beautiful face." "Maah-rokh" simply means a face like the moon, a beautiful face. "Zohreh jabeen" means "a face like Venus, or a beautiful face." The poet is using all the attributes he can think of to describe his beloved to create a sublime image in the mind of the reader. This repetition would never do in English, so I have left them alone.

[270] "My sweet heart."

[271] Thin, sickly thin.

[272] Hafez uses the word "estekhaareh," or "consulting a book, a holy writ, a poem, or even a rosary" to get answers to questions concerning the future. It is a kind of hesitation to consult God by some means before taking an action. As a matter of fact, for the Persian speaking world, Hafez is the most commonly used source for "estekhaareh," or "faal geeree."

[273] In few cases where Hafez has used the word "shahneh," which can be translated as "policeman," I have used judge, because "shahneh" has a different meaning from a policeman, a nuance that cannot be easily translated.

[274] The word Hafez uses is "jaameh morassa," or "gem studded cup," the idea indicating the value of the cup. I have used simply "gold" for the sake of poetic measure in English.

[275] Just a note to clarify the metaphor of "piercing pearls with the force of lashes": to be able to drink from the diamond studded cup of wine, you must cry many tears to obtain your objective.

[276] This may refer to a real garden, belonging to one of the patrons of Hafez, Shah Sheikh Abu Es-haagh. However, there is also a mention of such a garden in the Quran

[277] The word is "jaameh jahaan been," or "a cup that can see into the heart of the universe." I have used discerning as a summary.

[278] Hafez uses the word "khaamee," approximating "naivete" or "lack of experience and knowing."

[279] This word is hard to define, very much like "rendi." An "ayaar" is a clever, smart, rootless, sly, noble, unconventional person. Although developed independently, eventually "rendi" and "ayaari" collapsed into the same cluster of meanings. Perhaps, the word is best defined by its antonyms: virtuous, Sufi, ascetic, preacher and others. A reminder that Hafez uses these terms with distaste and disparagingly.

[280] Perhaps, a reference to the sprouting beard of a young lad.

[281] See note 76. The word is akin to "ayaar" in line four of this ghazal.

[282] See note 13. Additionally, when the signet was lost, Ahriman got hold of it for a while and abused it, until it was recovered by the will of God.

[283] Hafez uses "Ahriman," correctly translated as "Satan." However, the Persian "Sheytan" or "Satan" is not a very potent mythological character; he is often a funny one who is redeemable. "Ahriman" is evil incarnate, very much like the Judeo-Christian "Satan." For accuracy's sake, I have used the original word, which is also an English term.

[284] See note 165.

[285] One special kind of Persian white lily has five petals and five sepals, making ten strands in the shape of ten tongues, thus comparing, in a hyperbole, the possibility of Hafez's having ten tongues, much more articulate than having just one, but so sealed in awe that no words come out of his mouth in the presence of the beloved.

[286] In Islam eight different paradises are provisioned. I suspect, they might refer to the eight levels of paradise, not unknown, at least, among the Gnostics.

[287] See note 91.

[288] See note 76.

[289] See note 70.

[290] Perhaps a reference to Jacob, who slept in the desert with a stone to lay his head on (The Book of Genesis).

[291] Hafez uses the word "Khezr."

[292] Persian myth holds that the earth is balanced on the horns of a bull, and a new year arrives when the bull shifts the earth from one horn to another. However, the bull rests on the back of a fish. In this verse the idea is that the fish is at the lowest level of this cosmology and the moon at the highest. So, the reference is metaphorically to "from the lowest to the highest," a Persian poetic hyperbole. As a beggar, his realm is unbounded, from the earth to the heavens.

[293] See note 116.

[294] According to the Holy Book, Noah lived to be nine hundred fifty years.

[295] Here Hafez uses the word "kaam," "gratification." I have used "life" to be more direct.

[296] Ghol Ghand," a mixture of sugar and rose leaves, is a Persian folk remedy for weak heart. The poet objects that he will not be healed unless the lover offers her kisses and a few friendly insults as a matter of flirtation.

[297] The kind of clouds that come in the Persian month of Farvardeen (starting March 21), the first month of the year.

[298] Norooz, the most important feast, is the new year of the Persians, having millennial Zoroastrian history. It coincides with the first day of the spring.

[299] In old Persian tradition, a superior riding a horse, when he encounters an inferior, raises his whip and points towards the other person as a sign of affectionate recognition.

[300] In Persian poetic tradition, senses are often intermixed, so that one can hear a scent or taste a note of music. This is also done in the western tradition. Wallace Stevens, the twentieth century American poet, opts for such strategies. For a good example, see "Peter Quince at the Clavier." I quote five lines from the poem here:

> *Music is feeling, then, not sound;*
> *And thus it is that what I feel*
> *Here in this room, desiring you,*
> *Thinking of your blue-shadowed silk,*
> *Is music.*

[301] The *is* a reference to "peereh moghaan" or "Master," as I have translated it.

[302] Hafez uses the sentence "maa baadeh zeereh khergheh na emrooz meekhoreem" which literally means "We don't drink wine today under our garment!"

[303] There is a delicate double entendre here. A vat of wine, while fermenting, is sealed with mud for a duration. So, the second half of the line can be either read, "My lips are sealed and I am grieving in silence," or "The vat is sealed and the red wine like blood seethes itself into becoming robust and drinkable wine, all in silence."

[304] Another delicate ambiguity: either "I am trying to commit suicide," or "I am trying very hard at it!"

305 A reference to Adam, who ate from the forbidden fruit and was expelled from the Garden. An alternative myth proposes that the forbidden fruit was really "wheat," not "apple."

306 See note 51.

307 See note 9.

308 See note 223.

309 A bundle of roses is literally "seated" inside a container to extract the perfume which makes rose water. Does the poet compare his sweat to the scent of rose water?

310 Hafez uses the word "aragh-cheen," which is a kind of light hat worn in summers to keep sweat from the brows. Also, a cloth filter used in the extraction and making of rose water.

311 See note 158.

312 Perhaps, it is the month of Ramadan, the month of fasting for Moslems.

313 A reference to the city of Yazd in Iran. The literal meaning refers to Alexander the Great, whose prisons, the Persian remember, were filled with terror.

314 Hafez uses the word "Solomon," intending the province of Fars in southern Iran.

315 Here, Hafez uses an up-right, elegant juniper to refer to the beloved.

316 In traditional Persian writing, the pen employed was a length of reed, which was cut on one end with a notch cut through it so that the pressure of the writer's hand would make the shape of letters to conform to his style. In this line, the voice of his poem chooses to go as a reed pen with a notch that carries ink on the tip, representing bleeding heart and the suffering that it had to undergo to become a pen out of a piece of reed.

317 A reference to Arabs, possibly. I have kept the original word in my translation for the layers of metaphoric meaning that the word may carry.

318 A reference to the people of Faars or Paars; "paarsaa," a derivative, means "a man of integrity," in this line providing a double entendre. See also note 317.

319 See note 158.

320 Reference to wine: "we wash ...in wine."

[321] See note 91. I have a notion that this cup is similar to the Christian Holy Grail, which, also, reveals secrets.

[322] The word is "toheed," a belief in the One-ness of God and the unity of the creator. This is one of the main principles of Islam that the Holy Quran emphasizes: "I testify there is no God but One God."

[323] Nephew of Shah Shojaa, a patron of Hafez.

[324] He was a minor king and a nephew of Shah Shojaa, a favorite of Hafez,

[325] Meaning "the son of a Mogh (magi)," a wine steward in a tavern.

[326] Reference to old age, mansion being the body of age in which soul resides.

[327] Hafez uses the word "etaab," which cannot be directly translated into English. Incorporated in the deep meaning of the word are suggestions of anger, flirtation, and blame. The word is a bitter-sweet expression, which is not intended to be serious, but in the lover's lexicon, a temporary, but necessary encounter with feelings that contradict each other, and also complement each other.

[328] The day of resurrection.

[329] "Key" is the generic title of all the ancient Persian kings of the Keyaani dynasty.

[330] Reference to the cold month of Dey, which coincides with December (December 21st is Dey 1st.) It is the tenth month of the Persian calendar.

[331] A negation.

[332] See note 65.

[333] He was a classical man of great generosity and kindness. His name, Haatam Ibneh Abdolaah Ibneh Sad Ibn Alhashraai, is synonymous in the Islamic world with selfless giving.

[334] "Mann" is a measure of weight, almost three kilograms or a pound and half. Here, this hyperbole indicates the largest possible measure of wine to be drunk in honor of an extraordinary man of largess and generosity.

[335] Of course, this line directly connects with the previous verse, where the man demands a cup of wine "one mann" in weight. That amount of wine certainly cannot be absorbed and cleared through the normal process of biological systems, and the excess comes out in the form of sweat on the face.

[336] The months roughly in November and December. The idea is that when spring is available, meaning, youth, make the best of it because old age (Bahman and Dey) are relentlessly following you.

[337] See note 163.

[338] See notes 33, 329.

[339] The term used by Hafez is "jonnat al maavee," an area in the Garden where the Archangel Gabriel resides along with the righteous and other angels.

[340] See note 333.

[341] Musk is extracted from a gland in the belly of musk-deer. To obtain musk, the animal is "bloodied," (cut) in the belly (heart), but the deer is happy to donate the gift.

[342] This verse is in Arabic and alludes to Moses on the top of Mount Sinai, reflecting a small portion of God's luminosity from his face.

[343] See note 9 on Sedreh and Toobee.

[344] The lines address human soul, commenting that it is imprisoned in corporeal body, suggesting that it should go back to the Garden and fly to Toobee.

[345] This line is written in Arabic.

[346] Hafez, of course, means a person who has memorized (The Quran). It also means a protector, a mentor. May refer to the protector of the land and also to the Hafez of the land, the poet-man belonging to the city.

[347] Perhaps a reference to a school book, a representative of "learning" and scholarship, which Hafez did not particularly like. He equated scholars with the ascetic and sufis and preachers, for whom he had little regard.

[348] The quality and nature of being a Darvish.

[349] Obviously, the violin had not been invented at the time Hafez was writing; however, there was a precursor to the violin, "robaab" often translated as viol.

[350] The word "sugar" in the second half of the line refers to "sweetness of words Hafez writes and spreads with his reed, or a pen made of reed," the only writing instrument of the time, which enabled a writer to scratch on a piece of precious paper—or, skin—his words.

[351] See note 13.

[352] See note 125.

[353] The second "book" refers to the book where the deeds of Hafez are recorded in God's Heaven to be used in the day of judgement.

[354] The meaning is roughly this: "Like Alexander, I will acquire that Jaameh Jam (a vessel that holds wine with mirror-like reflective quality) from the Master. If I get drunk on it, or not, is immaterial." According to a Persian lore, Alexander employed mirrors to set on fire the wooden ships of his enemies by concentrating the rays of the sun on them.

[355] I assume the reference is to a polo ball and bat, which represent the firmament and the invisible bent bat that drives the ball of the wheel.

[356] This is obviously a homosexual reference, and a number of other poems of Hafez have this inference. A suggestion has been made that the use of feminine terms in the classical poetry of Iran is indecorous and indelicate. The oblique suggestion is that the term "lad," "boy," "Magi-boy," and others simply take the place of female references.

[357] The hometown of Hafez, a beautiful city that has been compared to the Garden of Eden. Hafez had a love affair with his native land and remained there most of his life, refusing big commissions from many monarchs in the Middle East. The city , to this day, has retained its charm and literary influence in whole of Iran.

[358] Or, Roknaabaad springs, still a famous water supply source.

[359] Traditional divisions of the earth, according to Persian mythology. Hafez is boasting that "the seven moles," (beauty marks) of the seven realms have been transferred to Shiraz.

[360] The pass is between two mountain peaks: Chehel Magaam and Baabaa Koohee, the head source of Roknaabaad brook. The literal meaning of the name is "God is Great."

[361] Perhaps a reference to Amir Mobaarez Al Deen, the king of the realm, who, in his fundamentalism, forbade drinking wine or playing musical instruments. No love was lost between Hafez and the king.

[362] The spout of the jug from which red wine (blood) pours into a cup.

[363] The title of an ancient, very just king of Iran, Anooshirvaaneh Aadel.

[364] A Sassanid king of an ancient dynasty of Iran.

[365] Different cities in vastly diverse geographical locations.

[366] The name of a school book that, probably, Hafez had read at school, operated by the funds provided through religious endowments.

[367] "Ogaaf" is a set of properties and funds that endowed a mosque or a group of mosques to operate schools and feed the needy. I have translated it as "Foundation."

[368] The fabulous mountains that surround the world. Perhaps, it is also a reference to the Caucasus mountains.

[369] Here is an oxymoron to show the gap between "rivals" and "companions" of the first half-line.

[370] Islamic law of hunting holds that no killing can be done inside the holy places.

[371] Hafez uses the Arabic word "mestabeh" or a raised platform in a mosque—or, any public place—for sitting and watching a performance. The closest word for it would be a balcony, a high platform (or, a dias).

[372] Traditional allusion to lips, laughing and smiling.

[373] The traditional six directions are front, back, left, right, up, and down. Hafez had created his own directions, using the tradition of Persian geography.

[374] In other words, "the curve of the brows of the beloved will conquer the pulpit of the Imam."

[375] "Pupil" becomes a representative of the beauty mark (Indian Mole), as if its reflection on the face is a real mole.

[376] Bahman is the son of the ancient king Afraasiyaab. Ghobaad was a famous Sassanid King of ancient Persia.

[377] Mythological kings of ancient Persia.

[378] See note 223.

[379] Perhaps this is the most troublesome of the ghazals that I have translated. I am not at all satisfied with the English text, but I have included it in the collection as an example of simple text, defying adequate translation from one language to another.

[380] The ninth scale of the twelve used in Persian music.

[381] Another scale. The import of the line, which is very complicated and contains a number of musical terms—not translated into English—is a doubt about the musician. Is he an imposter who starts his music in one scale and ends in another? If so, he is full of tricks, not to be trusted.

[382] Traditionally, Sufis wore their sleeves shorter as a sign of distinction. In contrast, Hafez describes the long arms because short sleeves allow their arms to look longer. However, the expression of "long hand" means cruelty and aggression and oppression. Thus, Hafez is criticizing those Sufis who brutalize people by the power they have accumulated through centuries. In general, Hafez was not very fond of Sufis.

[383] Perhaps the idea is that working only metaphorically is working with counterfeit and copies, metaphor being only a reflection of truth, rather than truth.

[384] The lexical meaning is "to listen"; however, in the Sufi tradition the word refers to singing and music that accompanies the dance of ecstasy.

[385] The Persian idiom, "kharman sookhteh," literally, a person whose grain harvest is burned, metaphorically means "ruined," thus, ruined Majnoon. On the literal level lightning sets a harvest gathered in a field on fire.

[386] See note 34.

[387] In a mystical vision, the natural self includes all the instinctual and animal characteristics. To achieve a higher degree of discernment, one must transcend this limitation and arrive at a higher understanding, which is mentioned in the second half of the line in the personification of "tareeghat" or "the way of life of the spirit and divine." A Jungian interpretation will be, if one desires individuation, one must be aware of the conscious self (natural), but must eventually go deep into the well-source of existence of "Self." Jung capitalizes Self to indicate a border between spirit and matter.

[388] In mystical terms, this means love, knowledge, and charity.

[389] In this line Hafez uses the word "aabeh roo" which could be read as tears or honor. Obviously this is a double meaning that cannot be translated into English.

[390] This is a famous Persian proverb.

[391] The Persian expression "aabeh rokhsaar" literally means "water of face," but in the idiom it refers to the features of a face; thus, the first half of this line could read "If Saghi's hand puts cosmetics on her face," or "splashes water-cosmetics on her face." The second half will confirm that, by doing so, many lovers will be heart broken, or bloodied, as if the face of Saghi is being painted on the blood of their hearts!

[392] A writ or an order from a king, sealed by his signet, signifying amnesty for life or property.

[393] Rendi is eternal and is ordained from the beginning to the end of the world, from eternity to eternity. The words "former" and "latter" refer to the full spectrum of time.

[394] Shabbaan is the month before the month of Ramazaan, the month of fasting for the Moslems all over the world. The Feast of Ramazaan is on the first day of the following month, Shavvaal. This calendar is lunar based, and the months do not coincide exactly with the rotation of the seasons.

[395] "Dey" is the tenth month in the Iranian calendar. Dey 1 is the first day of winter, coinciding with December 21.

[396] Here is a delicate metaphor: in winter all flowers die and only thorn remains. The thorn boasts of beauty until flower comes again and the thorn loses its glory. Truth always is revealed.

[397] Perhaps a reference to Shah Shojaa.

[398] I assume the reference is to making rose water or perfume from rose bundles by boiling and sweating them in special stills to distill the essence.

[399] A Zoroastrian angel who brings news, usually good news. Ahriman is the harbinger of evil news and is set against Ahura Mazda, God, an aspect of whom is in eternal conflict with Ahriman. In this line, perhaps the two divine elements complement, in a dialectics, to make a unity, which is the essence of the universe.

[400] A nightingale.

[401] An Eastern Turkic tribe, famous for bravery and the physical beauty of their people.

[402] A city in Western Turkmenistan, now a part of China.

[403] See note 13.

[404] See note 31.

[405] Reference to the dazzling light on Mount Sinai, where God revealed Himself to Moses in the form of flames and light. Of course, the fire did not burn Moses, who was safe and returned to bring the news to the Israelites.

[406] This line has been extensively revised to make sense in English. The original version is "You , who have a God-given beauty and the bridal chamber of luck----what need to bring a beautician in?"

[407] See note 125.

[408] This is the second month of the Persian calendar and the second month in spring, when the season has one foot in the warmth of late spring and one back in the winter.

BIBLIOGRAPHY

EDITIONS:

Divaane Hafez: Khajeh Shams-Al-Din Mohammad. 2 vols. 2nd edition. Edited and corrected by Parveez Natel Khanlari. Tehran: Entesharate Khaarazm, 1362. (Iranian Calendar)
  This edition lists 486 ghazals; it does not include an introduction or end-notes; however, Khanlari gives the collated account of each ghazal from different sources and editions immediately after each poem. For this reason, the set is valuable for authentication and correction. Any serious student of Hafez will find the book informative.

Divaane: Khajeh Shams-Al-Din Mohammad Hafeze Shirazi. Extensive color plates. Tehran: Ameer Kabeer, n.d.
  Gaudy color plates but beautiful calligraphy printed with lithographic process are the marks of this edition, a small, portable book, but not very reliable.

Hafez. Edited with introduction and notes by Mahmood Hooman. 3rd edition. Tehran: Tahroori Books, 1353. (Iranian Calendar)
  Hooman lists 248 ghazals, somewhat at variance with Khanlari and Khorramshahi. An impressive 100-page introduction provides general information about philosophical and poetic background, although with less success than Khorramshahi. At the end of the book, a 202-page discussion of Hafez's stylistics provides important information. This section also includes an essay on the process of collation and correction. The author provides notes for each poem.

Hafez Nameh. 2 vols. 9ᵗʰ edition. Edited with introduction and notes by Baha-al-Din Khorramshahi. Tehran: Sherkat-e Entesharat-e Elmi va Farhangi, 1378. (Iranian Calendar)

This book has been my best source of information and authentication. With its extensive notes at the end of each ghazal and a very impressive introduction and endnote commentaries, the book distinguishes itself above any other that I have consulted. The book lists 250 ghazals (I have translated 202) and includes a 300- page compendium of important information about each ghazal. For anyone who seeks a Persian edition for research, this book is a must. I am much indebted to Mr. Khorramshahi.

GENERAL:

Arberry, Anthony John. *Shiraz; Persian City of Saints and Poets.* Norman: University of Oklahoma Press, 1960.

_____. *Persian Poems, an Anthology of Verse.* Translations. Everyman's Library, No. 996. London: Dutton, 1954.

Browne, Edward Granville. *A Literary History of Persia.* 4 vols. 2ⁿᵈ edition, sixth printing. Bethesda, Maryland: Ibex Publishers, 1998.

Ghani, Ghassem. *Tareekheh Asreh Hafez* (A History of The Era of Hafez).Tehran: Ebn Sina, Booksellers, 1321, Iranian Calendar)

Basic Symbolic Images

Aaref: gnostic, wise, learned; used as a term of deprecation and sarcasm

Delbar: beloved, sweetheart

Doosh: dawn, early morning, yesternight

Homaa, homaay: phoenix, a dignified bird; a good omen

Narges: narcissus (flower), the eyes of the beloved

Nazar baazee: roaming eyes, ogling, flirting

Nightingale: For Hafez, this is the most used symbol for the "beloved," "lover." Since in the mystical poems the beloved equals God, then nightingale could metaphorically be read as God. It also refers to ecstasy, a lover's fever, eloquence in expression, an angelic voice bidding frivolity

Mogh: Magi

Mogh bacheh: young boy, a server in a tavern

Mohtaseb: bailiff, sheriff, judge, jailer

Peere Meyforoosh: the vintner, Master (see peere moghaan below)

Peere Moghaan: old Magi, Master, the voice of God

Ragheeb: rival, mentor, partner

Rend (-an): Until the time of Hafez, the word *rend* (*-an*, plural) characterized a person with low morality and of the lowest caste in the society, the butt of jokes for his higher, refined, spiritual and intellectual superiors. Hafez switches the meaning and applies "rend" to a person who is irreverent and a free-thinker. He is irreligious but has a great sense of the divine. He is gruff and irrational out-

wardly, but filled with sensitivity and kindness inside. He dispar-
ages the cleric, but he has a sense of the presence of God. If the
cleric are hypocritical, he is an honest, trustworthy man. He pos-
sesses equilibrium and follows the golden mean. This juxtaposition
provides Hafez with a sharper tongue to criticize the ruling classes
of his society on their own terms.

CORRESPONDENCE OF GHAZAL NUMBERS

For those wanting to read or compare with the original Persian (Khorram-shahi edition), the following chart gives the correspondence. In four instances Khorramshahi does not include the poem. In those instances the corresponding number of the Khanlari (KL) edition is given.

Ordoubadian	Khorramshahi	Ordoubadian	Khorramshahi
1	171	23	33
2	227	24	32
3	14	25	204
4	45	26	205
5	47	27	209
6	56	28	211
7	71	29	215
8	86	30	28
9	104	31	249
10	101	32	98
11	128	33	180
12	64	34	1
13	23	35	7
14	72	36	138
15	KL 46	37	149
16	36	38	150
17	126	39	155
18	8	40	174
19	213	41	201
20	67	42	202
21	82	43	31
22	77	44	200

Ordoubadian	Khorramshahi	Ordoubadian	Khorramshahi
45	89	75	113
46	85	76	112
47	48	77	246
48	236	78	13
49	4	79	12
50	3	80	11
51	2	81	18
52	KL 10	82	21
53	17	83	114
54	32	84	116
55	6	85	117
56	70	86	108
57	141	87	229
58	142	88	110
59	139	89	221
60	5	90	176
61	80	91	195
62	KL 247	92	189
63	29	93	186
64	191	94	140
65	105	95	147
66	51	96	148
67	225	97	151
68	KL 279	98	153
69	197	99	154
70	198	100	157
71	65	101	160
72	134	102	161
73	196	103	163
74	173	104	169

Ordoubadian	Khorramshahi	Ordoubadian	Khorramshahi
105	219	135	43
106	69	136	46
107	19	137	52
108	68	138	41
109	190	139	91
110	188	140	22
111	187	141	240
112	175	142	244
113	183	143	130
114	184	144	132
115	66	145	134
116	27	146	135
117	239	147	136
118	207	148	137
119	208	149	166
120	212	150	170
121	217	151	172
122	237	152	177
123	238	153	178
124	242	154	179
125	243	155	181
126	250	156	182
127	206	157	193
128	194	158	199
129	192	159	203
130	185	160	218
131	30	161	220
132	38	162	222
133	40	163	223
134	42	164	224

Ordoubadian	Khorramshahi	Ordoubadian	Khorramshahi
165	230	184	76
166	231	185	78
167	232	186	79
168	233	187	81
169	235	188	88
170	241	189	90
171	158	190	92
172	83	191	93
173	145	192	94
174	24	193	95
175	25	194	96
176	26	195	99
177	49	196	248
178	53	197	165
179	54	198	162
180	57	199	133
181	60	200	129
182	61	201	74
183	63	202	50

OTHER TITLES OF INTEREST FROM IBEX PUBLISHES

THE DIVAN-I HAFIZ / H. WILBERFORCE CLARKE TRANSLATOR
Complete literal translation of Hafez's divan with copious notes.
ISBN 0-936347-80-5

THE HAFEZ POEMS OF GERTRUDE BELL
ISBN 0-936347-39-2

IN WINESELLER'S STREET / THOMAS RAIN CROWE, TRANS.
Renderings of Hafez by American poet.
ISBN 0-936347-67-8

MILLENNIUM OF CLASSICAL PERSIAN POETRY / W. THACKSTON
Guide to the reading & understanding of Persian poetry from the10th to the 20th century
ISBN 0-936347-50-3

THE LOVE POEMS OF AHMAD SHAMLU / FIROOZEH PAPAN-MATIN
On the most popular modern Persian poet
ISBN 1-58814-037-7

SELECTED POEMS FROM THE DIVAN-E SHAMS-E TABRIZI
ISBN 0-936347-61-9

THE EYE OF AN ANT: PERSIAN PROVERBS & POEMS / F. AKBAR
Persian wisdom rendered into English verse along with the original
ISBN 0-936347-56-2

1001 PERSIAN-ENGLISH PROVERBS / SIMIN HABIBIAN
1001 Persian proverbs and idioms with corresponding English proverb and a literal translation in English. Illustrated.
ISBN 1-58814-021-0

A LITERARY HISTORY OF PERSIA / EDWARD G. BROWNE
The classic history of Persian literature
ISBN 0-936347-66-X

A HISTORY OF LITERARY CRITICISM IN IRAN / IRAJ PARSINEJAD
Literary Criticism in the Works of Akhundzadeh, Kermani, Molkom Khan, Talbof,
Maraghei, Kasravi and Hedayat
ISBN 1-58814-016-4

MODERN PERSIAN PROSE LITERATURE / HASSAN KAMSHAD
Classic on the subject and Hedayat with new introduction.
ISBN 0-936347-72-4

THE LITTLE BLACK FISH / SAMAD BEHRANGI
English translation and Persian text of mahi siah kuchulu.
ISBN 0-936347-78-3

AN INTRODUCTION TO PERSIAN / W. M. THACKSTON
A comprehensive guide and grammar to the language
ISBN 0-936347-29-5

HOW TO SPEAK, READ & WRITE PERSIAN / H. AMUZEGAR
A self-teaching course including book and audio cassettes.
ISBN 0-936347-05-9

PERSIAN-ENGLISH ENGLISH-PERSIAN LEARNER'S DICTIONARY
YAVAR DEHGHANI
18,000 entries. Persian words transliterated.
ISBN 1-58814-034-2

To order the above books or to receive
our catalog, please contact

Ibex Publishers / Post Office Box 30087 / Bethesda, MD 20824
Phone 301-718-8188 / Fax 301-907-8707 / www.ibexpublishers.com